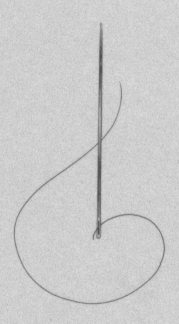

Painted with Thread: The Art of American Embroidery

Paula Bradstreet Richter, Curator of Textiles and Costumes

Peabody Essex Museum

Salem, Massachusetts

The front cover image is a detail from catalogue entry 60.

Peabody Essex Museum Collections for 2000
Volume 136
ISSN 1074-0457
ISBN 0-88389-119-0

The *Peabody Essex Museum Collections* is an annual monographic series published in Salem, Massachusetts.
All correspondence concerning this publication should be addressed to the Editor, *Peabody Essex Museum Collections,*
East India Square, Salem, Massachusetts 01970.
Previous books are available upon request. This volume was copyrighted in 2001 by the Peabody Essex Museum.

Unless otherwise noted, all photographs are from the collections of the Peabody Essex Museum.

Contents

Preface and Acknowledgments

In America, recognition of embroidery as an aesthetic medium has lagged behind the reappraisal and renewal of appreciation for other mediums formerly segregated into the realm of craft or decorative or folk art. A variety of circumstances account for this delay. Although the work of professional embroiderers has been available in America since the seventeenth century, a perception lingers that its primary practitioners have been schoolgirls and female hobbyists. Embroidery, as an aesthetic endeavor, whether practiced professionally or as an avocation, requires training that combines technical skill with instruction in aesthetics and design. Because embroiderers traditionally—and primarily—have been women, the appreciation of embroidery has fluctuated over time according to changes in the role of women in society and their relationships to the arts. The prevalence of patterns and kits has created a false impression that embroiderers are lacking in individual creativity and artistic expression. The use of embroidery on objects that combine aesthetic with functional purposes, such as clothing or domestic textiles, sometimes obscures the deeper meaning conveyed by these objects. Worse yet, the association of embroidery with sentimentalism and nostalgia has obscured some of the powerful messages that artists, past and present, have articulated through this medium.

The exhibition *Painted with Thread: The Art of American Embroidery* displays the art inherent in embroidered works made over the last several centuries. It interprets the artistic and cultural context of embroidery and the many ways in which artists and embroiderers have responded to the aesthetic movements that characterize different eras. The exhibition also highlights the timeless themes that the medium is uniquely suited to express. The exhibition recognizes the artistic contributions of many individuals and the vibrant evolving traditions that began centuries ago and continue unabated to the present day. In 1991, Lloyd E. Herman, the founding director of the Smithsonian's Renwick Gallery, made this comment about contemporary embroidery: "Art museums and galleries have slowly begun to recognize that art is not limited by medium, only by the individual artist's creative application of material and technique. But until art historians revise their texts to embrace the crafts, museums will continue to discriminate against art in fiber, wood, glass, clay and metal."[1] We hope that viewers of *Painted with Thread* will see embroidered works in a new light and thus be able to contribute to the ongoing dialogue about the arts in America.

The American Decorative Arts Department of the Peabody Essex Museum possesses an important collection of more than twenty-five thousand American textiles, costumes, and accessories. *Painted with Thread: The Art of American Embroidery* brings many works from this collection into public view for the first time. This collection and the textile collections from China, Japan, India, South Asia, the Pacific Islands, and Native America make the Peabody Essex Museum's textile holdings among the largest in the northeastern United States and of international significance. These hidden treasures will be exhibited on a regular basis as the museum expands its facilities and programming over the next several years.

The museum gratefully acknowledges the many individuals and organizations who have made this exhibition and publication possible. The museum received generous support for the exhibition from *PieceWork Magazine* and its publisher, Interweave Press. The Fund for American Costumes and Textiles, in memory of Anne Farnam, provided revenue used for the conservation of works in the exhibition. The Stevens Foundation provided a generous grant for textile conservation. Past participants in the museum's embroidery art symposium also made individual donations towards the conservation of embroideries featured in the exhibition. The Historic Needlework Guild gave a generous gift to produce the gallery guide for the exhibition.

The museum thanks Edward F. Maeder, the chair of the Curatorial Department and curator of textiles at Historic Deerfield, Massachusetts, and Dr. Laurel Thatcher Ulrich, the James Duncan Phillips Professor of History at Harvard University for serving as consultants for the review and planning of the exhibition. Betty Ring, the American needlework historian and author, generously agreed to write the foreword to this exhibition catalogue and shared information concerning object research. The following individuals and institutions provided research and other assistance to the museum's staff: Linda Behar; Ted Bonin of the Alexander and Bonin Gallery; Clare Browne and Elizabeth Currie of the Victoria and Albert Museum; Libby and Joanne Cooper of the Mobilia Gallery; Mary Fabiszewski of the Massachusetts Historical Society; David Kayser of the Salem Maritime National Historic Site of the National Park Service; Naomi Gray of the Phillips Trust House; Bruce Hackney of the Nicole Klagsbrun Gallery; Pamela Parmel of the Museum of Fine Arts, Boston; Karen Smith of the Carl Hammer Gallery; Michelle Tolini, a doctoral candidate at the Bard Graduate Center and a research assistant at the Costume Institute of the Metropolitan Museum of Art; Mark Tabbert of the Museum of Our National Heritage; and Donald Woodman and Susan Campbell of Through the Flower.

The scope of the exhibition has been expanded and greatly enhanced by loans of twentieth-century works from private individuals, artists, and institutions. They include: the Rene Breskin Adams, Albuquerque Museum, Emily Alexander and Robert Karron, Lou Cabeen, Dr. Irving Cooper, Dr. Stephanie Farber, Jay Jolly, Mr. and Mrs. Morris Larkin, Kynaston McShine, the Salem Maritime National Historic Site, and an anonymous lender. To each lender, we extend sincere thanks and deep appreciation for their contribution to this exhibition.

The museum is privileged to host internships for students from many academic institutions. Several students undertook projects related to this exhibition that made significant contributions to the exhibition catalogue and the installation of the exhibition. Elysa Engelman and Paul Schmitz of the American and New England Studies Program at Boston University did painstaking research on individual objects and their makers. Ms. Engelman's research unearthed the scandal at the Mrs. Rogers School in Salem, Massachusetts, in 1800 that she has developed into the case study that appears in this catalogue, beginning on page 141. (Ms. Engelman wishes to express her appreciation to William La Moy, Paula Richter, J. Rixie Ruffin, and the entire staff of the Phillips Library of the Peabody Essex Museum for their assistance.) Amanda Yost of Gordon College assisted with the computer cataloguing of the sampler and needlework collection. Tracey de Jong of Harvard University's Museum Studies Program did biographical research on embroiderers.

Several volunteers generously donated their time, skills, and enthusiasm to this exhibition. They included Jean Fallon, Carolyn Purcell, Hazel Trembley, Susanna Weld, and Catherine Wygant. Elwin Richter is warmly acknowledged for contributing the title to the exhibition and unwavering support of this project.

Many members of the staff of the Peabody Essex Museum contributed to the success of this project. The staff of the Phillips Library provided tireless assistance with research. Robert Segal and other members of the exhibition staff were responsible for the superb exhibition design and installation. Lucy Butler, Carrie Gervais, and Kristen Weiss managed object lists, loans, conservation, and installation of the exhibition. Carrie Gervais and Elizabeth Lahikainen coordinated a team of textile conservators who provided conservation services for the exhibition, including Deborah Bede, Irena Calenescu, Kathy Francis, T. Rose Holdcraft, and the staff of the Textile Conservation Center in Lowell, Massachusetts. Jeffrey Dykes, Markham Sexton, Heather Shanks, and Marc Teatum of the photography department provided superb photographic illustrations for the catalogue. William La Moy and Louise Sullivan copyedited the manuscript and oversaw the production of the catalogue. Media coordinators Christy Sorenson and Mark Keene produced multimedia components for the exhibition. Members of the education department produced the gallery guide and the group tour, travel, and interpretive programming. Other staff members who contributed time and expertise to this project included Susan Bean, Penny Bigmore, Anne Cademenos, Karina Corrigan, Mary Lou Curran, Jennifer Evans, Daniel Finamore, Lynne Francis-Lunn, Rae Francoeur, John Grimes, Frederick McDougall Johnson, Dean Lahikainen, Greg Liacos, William Phippen, Karl Rosenberger, Martha Rush-Mueller, Lisa Senchyshyn, Tamsen Snyder, and Allyson Stanford.

Dan L. Monroe
Executive Director
Peabody Essex Museum

Foreword

This exhibition is a joyous celebration of the extraordinary richness of needlework treasures owned or produced on the North Shore of Massachusetts for more than two centuries. Fortunately, that incomparable diarist the Reverend William Bentley (1759–1819) provided a uniquely intimate history of the citizens of Salem and its environs, but much evidence of women's lives and education in early America was written with a needle. Happily, these sources now blend to expand the knowledge of women's and men's lives in the exceptionally vigorous settlements of this region.

The artifacts we find here clearly reflect the foresight of the founders of the very early institutions that ultimately became the Peabody Essex Museum. From their beginnings, they obviously inspired confidence, and consequently received artifacts, books, and manuscripts that have made this presentation so visually appealing and exceptionally informative.

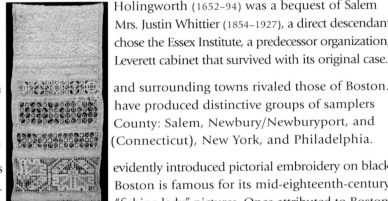

Here we see the girlhood sampler of Anne Gower Endicott (ca. 1610), which was surely the earliest sampler to come to America, while the splendid work of Salem's Mary Holingworth (1652–94) was a bequest of Salem antiquarian George Rea Curwen (1823–1900). In 1925, Mrs. Justin Whittier (1854–1927), a direct descendant of Massachusetts governor John Leverett (1616–79), chose the Essex Institute, a predecessor organization, as the proper place for the seventeenth-century Leverett cabinet that survived with its original case.

In the eighteenth century, the girls' schools of Salem and surrounding towns rivaled those of Boston. In fact, only eight American towns are known to have produced distinctive groups of samplers during the colonial period, and three were in Essex County: Salem, Newbury/Newburyport, and Haverhill. The others were Boston, Newport, Norwich (Connecticut), New York, and Philadelphia.

In addition to fine samplers, a Salem schoolmistress evidently introduced pictorial embroidery on black silk about a decade before it appeared in Boston. Boston is famous for its mid-eighteenth-century pastoral embroideries in canvas work often called "fishing lady" pictures. Once attributed to Boston schools, it now appears likely that bucolic scenes by schoolgirls such as those by Sarah Chamberlain and Anne Ward were worked at Salem schools because the pieces that most closely resemble their embroideries were also worked by Salem girls. Indeed, Essex County schools produced outstanding needlework during the colonial and Federal periods.

In addition to early American embroideries, the museum has also collected works of the nineteenth and twentieth centuries and actively collects historical and contemporary works today. These later works include Berlin wool work, embroideries influenced by the Arts and Crafts movement, Colonial Revival pieces of the twentieth century, and works by contemporary artists. The museum presents this remarkable American embroidery from the seventeenth century to the present in the exhibition *Painted with Thread: The Art of American Embroidery*.

Betty Ring
30 January 2001

Introduction

When an embroiderer selects a colored filament, threads a needle, and takes the first stitch into a pristine piece of cloth, a process of artistic creation and transformation begins. Simple materials—thread and cloth—when combined by an artist of vision and skill, produce works that are beautiful, that express ideas, and that communicate personal and cultural messages. Embroidery is inherently an aesthetic act. Although highly regarded as an aesthetic medium in Europe and Asia, the practice of embroidery in America is often relegated to the status of a minor domestic craft or hobby. Perhaps it is because embroidery can be applied to functional objects, or is sometimes done with the aid of commercial patterns and kits, or that people practice it as a means of relaxation, that its significance within the context of art has yet to be adequately explored. The consideration of embroidery as an art form brings issues and biases about art into focus and adds to the ongoing dialogue about what constitutes art.

The exhibition entitled *Painted with Thread: The Art of American Embroidery* explores the topic of embroidery as a means of artistic and cultural expression. It displays a broad spectrum of embroidery as art, craft, fine art, folk art, interior decoration, fashion, and as a means of communication. It explores the lives of artists who embroider, whether they practice the medium as a vocation or as a hobby. It considers original and personal uses of embroidery as well as those derived or adapted from prevalent artistic styles and movements. It includes works by a diverse group of people over more than three centuries, including contemporary artists who push the boundaries of embroidered art in new directions.

Embroidery is currently experiencing a revival of popularity at multiple levels. In recent years, American samplers and needlework have realized record-setting prices at auction.[1] Embroidery and related needle crafts are among the most popular pastimes now practiced by Americans seeking relief in this quiet meditative activity from the stress and fast pace of contemporary life.[2] Embroidery has also found new uses in the hands of contemporary artists who draw inspiration from ancient techniques and forms but move beyond the past and explore new avenues of expression at the beginning of this new millennium.[3]

Painted with Thread: The Art of American Embroidery presents a selection of approximately one hundred objects from the Peabody Essex Museum's rich holdings in American textiles and embroidery art. Drawn from several of the museum's departments, this selection features works made or used in America from the seventeenth century to the present day. The objects reflect the regionalism of the museum's American decorative arts collection that focuses on New England and the northeastern United States with a concentration on the North Shore of Massachusetts. However, the exhibit also includes works made abroad, including pieces made in England, Europe, and Asia that have documented American provenance or history of use. This reflects the museum's international collecting initiatives as well as the reality that Americans have owned imported goods as well as those made domestically since the beginning of the colonial period. The exhibition is not intended as a comprehensive treatment of the subject of American embroidery but rather focuses on one institution's collections. The exhibition also features twentieth-century works borrowed from private and institutional collections that show the diverse and dynamic ways that contemporary artists use embroidery in the creation of art at the present time and recent past.

Founded in 1799, the museum's parent organization, the East India Marine Society, established "a museum of natural and artificial curiosities from beyond the Capes," reflecting international maritime trade to ports beyond the Cape of Good Hope and Cape Horn. The society began collecting textiles, including embroidered works, in the early nineteenth century drawn from around the world, but also reflecting interest in regional

American history and culture. Among the earliest pieces displayed at the museum was the sampler (1610–20) worked by Anne Gower, wife of Governor John Endicott, that was deposited at the museum of the East India Marine Society in 1828 by an Endicott descendant (catalogue entry 1).

This interest in American art, history, and culture intensified in the nineteenth century with the approach of the centennial celebration in 1876. The Essex Institute, a regional historical society formed in 1821 and a second parent organization of the present museum, hosted the *Exhibition of Antique Relics* in 1875 to raise money for the Centennial Exhibition in Philadelphia, the first world's fair held in the United States. Sponsored by the Salem Ladies Centennial Committee, the exhibition displayed approximately six hundred objects of historical interest assembled from private family collections in addition to the museum's holdings. Among the objects on display was the Leverett family's seventeenth-century embroidered cabinet (see catalogue entry 3) that was eventually donated to the museum over fifty years later.

In 1893, the Essex Institute and the Peabody Academy of Science joined forces to create the museum's first large-scale traveling exhibition. It was sent to the World's Columbian Exposition in Chicago, a world's fair that commemorated the four-hundredth anniversary of the arrival of Christopher Columbus in America. Among the exhibits housed in the reception rooms of the Massachusetts State Building was a case of "Old-time needlework" that included samplers made by Anne Gower (catalogue entry 1) and Nabby Mason Peele (catalogue entry 14). These early exhibitions must have attracted the attention of the collectors and authors who pioneered scholarship on the subject of American samplers and needlework. Works from the Essex Institute appeared in several important monographs of the early twentieth century, including *American Samplers* (1921) by Ethel Stanwood Bolton and Eva Johnston Coe, Candace Wheeler's *Development of Embroidery in America* (1921); and Georgiana Brown Harbeson's *American Needlework* (1938). While these events represent the very beginnings of the museum's acquisitions and display of American embroidery, it would be misleading to suggest that the museum considered embroidery as a primary collecting area in the past. Many embroidered objects came into the museum's collections as part of large assemblages of family collections, as decorative items associated with historic houses and domestic interiors, or in association with textile and clothing collections. Recently, the collecting goals for the American textile and costume collection have been reaffirmed and expanded, and this exhibition presents several recent acquisitions and many items that have not been exhibited or discussed in print previously.

In the twentieth century, the museum occasionally exhibited embroidered objects in small displays or included individual objects in decorative arts exhibitions. *Painted with Thread: The Art of American Embroidery* is the first exhibition that surveys the breadth of the collection and that is accompanied by a catalogue. Sixty-eight of the objects in the exhibition have been selected for extended catalogue entries and are organized chronologically so that this publication can serve as a general guide to the collection. The exhibition, however, is organized into six sections that present this diverse body of embroidered objects in thematic groupings. Brief summaries of the six sections appear below. The checklist of the exhibition that follows includes all of the works in the show and reflects the organizational groupings of the installation.

When working with museum collections, curators and others often experience the joy of encountering beautiful and deeply meaningful objects. As you turn the pages of this catalogue or visit the exhibition, it is hoped that these objects will move you with the same sense of delight and appreciation.

Paula Bradstreet Richter
Curator of Textiles and Costumes
Peabody Essex Museum

Checklist of the Exhibition

The Artists and Their Work

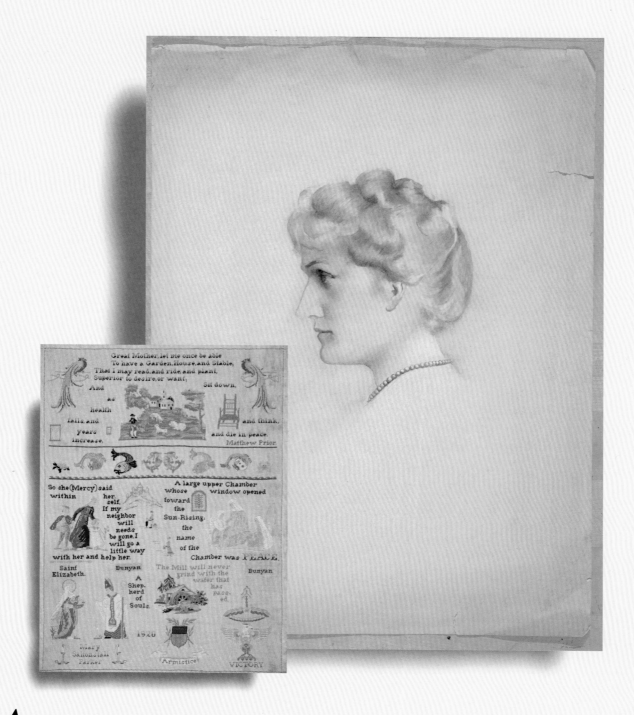

An introductory section of the exhibition features works by five artists—an eighteenth-century schoolgirl, a Victorian embroiderer, a Colonial Revival needlework designer of the early twentieth century, a mid-twentieth-century artist, and a contemporary artist—each accompanied by their portraits. The intent of this arrangement is to focus on the connection between the art object and its maker. The works demonstrate the variety of styles, techniques, and cultural contexts of embroidery over a broad expanse of time that are represented in the exhibition. The artists' portraits present the individual behind the artwork and introduce the theme of artists' biographies that will be explored periodically throughout the exhibition.

Schoolgirl Needle Arts

*R*ecalling her childhood experiences in Newburyport, Massachusetts, in the early nineteenth century, Sarah Anna Emery wrote that "One was considered very poorly educated who could not exhibit a sampler." Probably the best known surviving embroideries from early America are samplers and pictorial needlework done by schoolgirls as part of their formal educational curriculum. In the seventeenth, eighteenth, and nineteenth centuries, schoolmistresses provided instruction in plain sewing and ornamental embroidery techniques that were later utilized in the creation and maintenance of clothing and household textiles. In addition to functional skills and vocational training, embroidery also involved varying levels of art instruction that exposed students to prevalent artistic styles, elements of design, and craftsmanship. Ornamental embroidery could be as rudimentary as a simple floral vine on the first sampler completed by an eight-year-old student. Alternatively, embroidery works could be described, as Sarah Emery did, as "large and elaborate specimens of handiwork; framed and glazed, they often formed the chief ornament of the sitting room or best chamber."[7] Included in this section are works from renowned New England schools such as the Saunders and Beach Academy in Dorchester, Massachusetts, or significant local schools such as that kept by Mistress Sarah Stivours of Salem.

The creation of samplers and pictorial needlework taught more than reading, sewing, and art; they also reinforced gender roles and prevalent ideas about morality, cultural values, and religion. The charm and elegance of these works sometimes belie the complex messages embodied in them and the cultural context in which they were created. For example, the embroidered coats of arms done in the eighteenth century made visual statements about family identity, gentility, status, and affluence (catalogue entries 15 and 19). Painted and embroidered scenes such as *Cornelia and the Graachi* (catalogue entry 33 and the image above) display the aesthetics of classical antiquity and also the ideals of "republican motherhood" in the early years of American democracy. The complexities and controversies inherent in women's education in early America erupted in Salem in 1800 when a scandal surrounding a schoolmistress and her pupils spilled into the newspapers and polarized local citizens. The case study on the Abigail Rogers school of Salem described by Elysa Engelman in this publication explores this event and the social and cultural background of female education in New England during the Federal period.

27 *Painted and embroidered allegorical picture* (1804)
by Maria Crowninshield (1789–1870)
Dorchester, Massachusetts
Silk, watercolor, metallic thread, and reverse painting on glass; 24³/₄ x 19¹/₄ in.
Gift of Mr. and Mrs. Francis B. Lothrop, 1980
M18627

12 *Sampler* (1774)
by Elizabeth Derby (1762–1814)
Salem, Massachusetts
Silk and linen; 15¹/₂ x 10³/₄ in.
Gift of Louisa Lander, 1894
3543

14 *Sampler* (1778)
by Nabby Mason Peele (1767–1834)
Salem, Massachusetts
Silk and linen; 15¹/₂ x 19 in.
Gift of Mary T. Saunders, 1890
109643

17 *Sampler* (1788)
by Sally Rust (1776–1803)
Salem, Massachusetts
Silk and linen; 21¹/₄ x 20¹/₂ in.
Museum purchase with funds donated anonymously, 1995
137741

21 *Sampler* (ca. 1800)
by Sally Martin Bowen (1789–1872)
Marblehead, Massachusetts
Silk and linen; 20¹/₈ x 16¹/₄ in.
Gift of Frederick W. Story Sr., 1981
135370

28 *Sampler* (1806)
by Elizabeth Briggs (1796–1866)
Salem, Massachusetts
Silk and linen; 24⁵/₈ x 23¹/₄ in.
Gift of Elizabeth Wheatland, 1897
3846 (109716)

30 *Sampler* (1807)
by Sarah Todd (b. 1798)
Northeastern Massachusetts or New Hampshire
Silk and linen; 26 x 25¹/₂ in.
Gift of Philip T. Andrews, 1977
133922

37 *Sampler* (1822)
by Sarah Prescott (1813–1909)
Westford (Forge Village), Massachusetts
Silk and linen; 12³/₈ x 12¹/₄ in.
Gift of the estate of Grace Lawrence, 1936
122669

19 *Embroidered coat of arms* (1797) *of the Peirce family*
by Sarah Peirce (1780–1835)
Salem, Massachusetts
Silk, metallic thread, and metal spangles; 17³/₈ x 17³/₈ in.
Gift of the estate of Charlotte Sanders Nichols, 1935
FIC1688

33 *Cornelia and the Gracchi* (1808)
by Lydia Very (1792–1867)
Salem, Massachusetts
Silk, paint, and metallic thread; 17¹/₂ x 22³/₄ in.
Gift of the estate of Lydia L. A. Very, 1906
100507

Purse and belt (1825–35)
by Sarah Prescott (1813–1909)
Massachusetts
Glass, silk, and cotton; purse: 9³/₄ x 7 in.; belt: 1³/₄ x 24 in.
Gift of Grace Lawrence, 1935
122255.A, B

35 *Worktable* (1820–21)
by Mary L. Poor (1806–84)
North Shore of Massachusetts
Maple, birch, paint, and brass; 29 x 19¹/₂ x 15 in.
Museum purchase, 1982
135590

29 *Cymbeline* (ca. 1807)
by Mehitable Neal (1786–1856)
Dorchester, Massachusetts
Silk, paint, glass, wood, and gilding; 17 x 22¹/₂ in.
Museum purchase with funds donated anonymously, 1997
137797

Engraving of scene II from act I of **Cymbeline** (1793)
by Thomas Burke after a painting by William Hamilton and published by John and Josiah Boydell
London
Ink on paper; 21¹/₂ x 29⁷/₈ in.
Gift of F. Lee Eiseman, 1993
137668.2

Specimens of needlework (ca. 1836) *executed at the Female Model School, Kildare Place, Dublin*
Ireland
Paper, silk, linen, and other materials; 9 x 12 in.
Gift of C. Bertha Dobson, 1924
117694

Pincushions and box
(late eighteenth or early nineteenth century)
by Phoebe Griffen (1734–1829)
New England
Silk, linen, and paper; 6¹/₂ x 1¹/₄ in.; 9 x 2³/₈ in.; 2⁷/₈ x 7³/₄ in.
Gift of Mrs. G. W. Winthrop, 1948
127632; 127633

Miniature pocket and needle case
(late eighteenth or early nineteenth century)
probably by Eliza Abby Cleveland (1802–36) or Abigail Cleveland (1759–1834)
Linen, silk, and metallic thread; pocket: 4¹/₈ x 3³/₄ in.; needle case: 3¹/₂ x 2 in.
Gift of the Cleveland estate, 1919
108347; 108362

Blanket (ca. 1830)
by Sarah Prescott (1813–1909) and Olive Prescott (1780–1860)
Forge Village (Westford), Massachusetts
Wool; 68 x 90 in.
Gift of Grace Lawrence, 1914
104495

1 *Sampler* (1610–20)
by Anne Gower (d. 1629)
England
Linen; 17 x 7 in.
Gift of Captain Samuel J. Endicott, 1918
106842

3 *Embroidered cabinet and case* (1655–85)
attributed to the daughters of Governor John Leverett
New England or England
Silk, linen, metallic thread, wood, gilding, gesso, and brass; 12 x 10⁷/₈ x 7¹/₂ in.
Gift of Mrs. Justin Whittier, 1925
118284

16 *Embroidered coat of arms* (ca. 1784) *of the Fisk family*
by Lydia Fisk (1768–85)
Boston, Massachusetts
Silk, metallic thread, and metal spangles; 18³/₈ x 18³/₈ in.
Bequest of the Misses Allen, 1920
112131

Boston Harbour (1800)
by Sally Dodge
Medford, Massachusetts
Silk and paint; 23 x 19 in.
Loaned anonymously

Sailors' Embroidery

*B*ritish and American sailors learned rudimentary sewing techniques in order to make and repair sails, clothing, and other textile objects on board ship during voyages that could last for many months or even years. While at sea, sailors were freed from the prevailing social constraints of the nineteenth century that associated sewing with women. Some seamen also utilized sewing and embroidery as a recreational occupation, one of a number of crafts such as scrimshaw, macramé, wood carving, and ship modeling now considered maritime folk art. Embroidered ship portraits called "woolies" were the most prevalent form of sailors' needlework that survives. Sailors created these stitched replicas of vessels as mementos for loved ones while they were away from home or in retirement as nostalgic reminders of their years at sea. Until the mid-nineteenth century, seamen were also responsible for providing and maintaining their own clothing. Seamen sometimes embellished garments to be worn on shore leave such as the sailor's embroidered pants (catalogue entry 40 and above). In addition to these sailor-artists, professional artists such as Thomas Willis of New York created extraordinary "silk pictures" of ships in the late nineteenth century that are easily mistaken for paintings at a glance.

40 *Sailor's pants* (1830–50)
by an unidentified artist on a voyage from
New England to the Pacific Ocean
Wool, cotton, linen, and wood; length:
42 in.; waist: 32$\frac{1}{2}$ in.
Gift of Sarah V. G. Peck, 1954
128941

Ship **Hoogley** *of Boston* (nineteenth century)
attributed to Thomas Willis (1850–1912)
United States
Paint, silk, cotton, canvas, and pencil;
24$\frac{1}{2}$ x 32$\frac{1}{2}$ in.
Gift of Mrs. Samuel K. Lothrop, 1983
M20468

42 *Embroidered ship portrait or "woolie"*
(mid-nineteenth century)
by an unidentified artist
United States, probably New England
Cotton, silk, and canvas; 17$\frac{1}{2}$ x 23$\frac{3}{4}$ in.
Gift of Mrs. Henry Vaughan, 1945
M5706

Embroidered ship portrait or "woolie"
(nineteenth century)
by an unidentified artist
Probably England
Wool and canvas; 20$\frac{1}{4}$ x 26$\frac{1}{2}$ in.
Gift of the estate of George G. Kirstein, 1986
M22387

50 *Ship* **Marianne Nottebon** *of New York*
(late nineteenth century)
attributed to Thomas Willis (1850–1912)
New York
Oil paint, cotton, silk, and canvas;
26$\frac{1}{4}$ x 38 in.
Gift of Gladys and Emily Safford, 1952
M6663

Sea bag (late nineteenth century)
by an unidentified artist
United States
Cotton; 53$\frac{7}{8}$ x 22$\frac{1}{2}$ in.
Loaned by the Salem Maritime National
Historic Site of the National Park Service

Sailor's ditty box (ca. 1849)
owned by John Putnam
New England
Wood, cotton, silk, leather, and paper; 3 x 6 in.
Gift of Professor Albert Bushnell Hart, 1929
M3476

Home

Among the most ubiquitous of Victorian embroideries was the motto "Home, Sweet Home" stitched in brightly colored wool on perforated paper. For centuries, the home has served as a canvas on which embroiderers have manifested diverse aesthetic and cultural expressions. The intersection of function and aesthetics is readily apparent in embroidered objects made for use in the context of domestic interiors. For this reason, they are sometimes overlooked in the consideration of embroidery as an art form. These objects, however, provide evidence about how people incorporate art into everyday life and personal environments. Cultural beliefs about women and home management have directed their artistic impulses in particular to the embellishment, personalization, and improvement of the home. Not only has this included their consumer choices of purchased commercial goods but also the creation of embellished functional objects and fancywork handmade for the home. The objects in this section include bed hangings, tablecloths, furniture, upholstery, needlework tools and equipment, and other embroidered household textiles. In addition to functional objects, works of contemporary art explore conceptual ideas about home and domestic life.

43 *Packet of silk thread stamped "Linhing"* (ca. 1840)
China
Paper and silk; 25 x 15 in.
Gift of the Massachusetts Society of Colonial Dames of America, 1980
E82207

Needle case (1830–50)
by an unidentified artist
United States
Silk, wool, and paper; 4^1/$_4$ x 3^1/$_2$ in.
Gift of Robert B. Williams, 1970
132295

Needle case (1862)
by Lily P. Kenny and Mary E. Kenny
Salem, Massachusetts
Wool, silk, glass, paper, and cardboard; 5^1/$_2$ x 3 in.
Gift of Beatrice A. Brown, 1961
130001

62 *Original art work for needlework patterns* (1910–15)
by Jenny Brooks (1866–1937)
Salem, Massachusetts
Watercolor, ink, pencil, and paper; 13 x 10 in.
Gift of Mrs. Peter Shyte, 1963
130217

45 *Table cover and table* (1840)
*by Mary Berry True (1788–1858)
and Joseph True (1785–1873)*
Wool, cotton, and mahogany; 30^3/$_4$ x 28^1/$_2$ in.
Salem, Massachusetts
Gift of Mrs. Arthur T. Wellman, 1974
133540; 133541

47 *Fire screen* (1845–60)
by Mary Hodges (Cleveland) Allen (1817–73)
Salem, Massachusetts
Wool, silk, and mahogany; 59 x 24 in.
Bequest of Marion C. and Elizabeth C. Allen, 1913
103712

53 *Mantel valance* (1875–95)
by an unidentified artist
New England
Wool; 11 x 52 in.
Gift of Miss E. Evans, 1928
119651

11 *Valence from a set of bed hangings* (ca. 1770)
by the Eveleth family
North Shore of Massachusetts
Wool and linen; 83^1/$_8$ x 13 in.
Gift of Mrs. Fannie P. Rust, 1918
107291

Chair with needlework upholstery (ca. 1859)
by Henrietta Augusta (Saunders) Coolidge (1838–1926)

New England, probably Boston, Massachusetts
Wool, canvas, and mahogany; 35 x 15^3/$_4$ x 15 in.
Gift of Mrs. Willard B. Dik, 1978
134337

34 *Windsor stools with needlework upholstery* (1810–30)
by an unidentified artist
New England
Painted pine, wool, silk, linen, and brass; 15 in.
Museum purchase, Fendelman Collection, 1993
137665.2AB

41 *Sewing table* (ca. 1835)
by an unidentified artist
China
Lacquer on wood, ivory, and silk; 28^7/$_8$ x 24 x 16^3/$_8$ in.
Gift of Mr. and Mrs. Francis B. Lothrop, 1970
E82997

Sewing box (1820–40)
by an unidentified artist
New England
Mahogany, ivory, and silk; 7 x 7 x 5^1/$_2$ in.
Gift of Miss M. B. Perkins, 1921
112863

Work box (ca. 1815)
painted by Hannah Crowninshield (1789–1834)
Salem, Massachusetts
Mahogany, maple, pine, and watercolor; 4 x 12 x 9 in.
Gift of the Misses Elizabeth L. and Katherine F. Clark, 1957
M9331 (130098)

Lamp mat (1825–50)
by an unidentified Huron or Tuscarora artist
Northeastern United States
Wool, moose hair, and pigment; 11 x 11 in.
Gift of Willis H. Ropes, 1931
E20836

57 *Banner screen* (1875–1900)
by Mrs. Nathaniel A. (Harriet M.) Horton (1832–1908)
Salem, Massachusetts
Silk, wool, and brass; 26 x 12 in.
Gift of William A. Horton, 1921
113969

51 *Panel for a fire screen* (1865–85)
by an unidentified artist
Salem, Massachusetts
Wool, glass, metal, and cotton; 31^1/$_2$ x 28 in.
Gift of Edward D. Lovejoy, 1946
122921

52 *Chair seat upholstery* (1865–85)
by an unidentified artist
Probably Salem, Massachusetts
Wool, cotton, and glass; 21^1/$_2$ x 22 in.
Gift of Edward D. Lovejoy, 1946
122920

54 *Valance* (1875–85)
by an unidentified artist
New England
Wool, linen, silk, and glass beads; 14 x 21^1/$_4$ in.
Gift of Mrs. Shepard D. Gilbert, 1945
126547

13 *Table cover* (1779)
by Susannah Hiller (1751?–1822)
Salem or Boston, Massachusetts
Silk and linen; 26^1/$_2$ x 19^1/$_2$ in.
Bequest of Annie Regina Foster, 1949
127945

58 *Table cover* (1885–95)
by an unidentified artist
New England
Silk, metallic thread, and cotton; 60^1/$_2$ x 61^1/$_2$ in.
Gift of Ellen Moulton, 1944
125860

56 *Table cover* (1870–80)
by Mrs. Josiah (Eliza Tufts) Brodhead (1831–1900)
Probably Boston, Massachusetts
Silk and wool; 62 x 62 in.
Gift of Mrs. Paul T. Haskell, Mrs. John Pickering, and Mrs. James J. Storrow, 1960
129730

60 *Set of doilies* (1899–1905)
by Mable Clare Hillyer Pollock (1884–1963)
Ohio or Massachusetts
Silk on linen; 15 and 9 in. in diameter
Gift of the estate of Mable Clare Hillyer Pollock, 1963
130484.1–4

A Man's Home Is His Castle (1994)
by Matthew Benedict (b. 1968)
United States
Cotton; 12 x 20 in.
Loaned by Kynaston McShine

Blank Page, Mental Buzz (1983)
by Rene Breskin Adams
United States
Cotton; 19 x 15^1/$_4$ in.
Loaned by the artist

Sampler (The Little Work-Tables) (1996)
by Elaine Reichek
United States
Cotton and linen; 19 x 19^1/$_4$ in.
Loaned by Stephanie Farber

Ambition (1997)
by Lou Cabeen
United States
Found family textiles; 18 x 48 in.
Loaned by the artist

Nature

An eighteenth-century sampler verse begins with the expression "Here in this green and shady bower." Elements of the natural world have been a source of inspiration for embroidery for centuries. The beauty of landscapes, gardens, and animal and floral motifs have been used to express ideas about utopia, human relationships and identities, and beliefs about the relationship between the natural world and mankind. For example, in the eighteenth century, the pastoral landscape of English country estates was adapted in colonial America as an expression of refinement and gentility. In the nineteenth century, flowers and plant life were codified as a symbolic language used to express romantic and sentimental ideals. The Victorian "language of flowers" was utilized by artists to add layers of meaning to their work and was a particular favorite with embroiderers. Native American artists utilized indigenous traditions sometimes intermingled with Europeanized depictions of landscapes and floral motifs in moose hair and with various embroidery techniques to produce trade goods and souvenirs that are also works of art. Contemporary works demonstrate constantly evolving views of nature and the environment and also the ongoing inspiration that the natural world provides to artists.

10 *Sampler* (1764)
by Elizabeth Herbert (1751–67)
Salem, Massachusetts
Silk, metallic thread, and linen;
17³/₄ x 14¹/₂ in.
Gift of Mrs. Percival Foster, 1981
M19027

15 *Sampler* (1783)
by Mary Richardson (1772–1824)
Salem, Massachusetts
Silk and linen; 24¹/₄ x 23¹/₂ in.
Gift of Lucy L. Caller, 1938
123559

5 *Pastoral canvas-work picture* (1735–50)
by Sarah Ropes (1717–90)
Salem, Massachusetts
Wool, silk, and linen; 11 x 9 in.
Gift of Charlotte S. Nichols, 1936
133428

7 *Pastoral canvas-work picture* (ca. 1765)
by Sarah Chamberlain (1750–96)
Boston or Salem, Massachusetts
Wool, silk, linen, and metallic thread;
8³/₈ x 10 in.
Gift of Mary B. Chamberlain, 1951
128281

8 *Pastoral canvas-work picture* (1760–65)
by Anna Ward Mansfield Henfield (1744–1832)
Salem or Boston, Massachusetts
Wool, silk, linen, and paint; 15¹/₄ x 23³/₄ in.
Gift of Ethel Hammond, 1947
126995

9 *Pastoral canvas-work picture* (1750–80)
by an unidentified artist
Salem or Boston, Massachusetts
Wool, silk, and linen; 11⁵/₈ x 14³/₄ in.
Gift of Mrs. Edward Law, 1941
124819

31 *Embroidered picture* (1800–1810)
by Maria Chever (1789–1868)
Probably Salem, Massachusetts
Silk, reverse painting on glass, wood, and
gilding; 20¹/₂ x 17¹/₂ in.
Gift of the estate of Sarah A. Chever, 1908
101801

32 *The Dance* (ca. 1815)
by Frances Leverett from Oliver Goldsmith's
"The Deserted Village"
Boston or the North Shore of Massachusetts
Silk, watercolor, and chenille; 17 x 23 in.
Gift of the estate of Clifton Winsor White
in memory of his mother, Sarah Shays
White, 1960
129212

46 *Embroidered dog portrait* (1840–60)
by an unidentified artist
United States
Wool, cotton, and glass; 26 x 25 in.
Gift of an anonymous donor, 1919
109449

39 *Apron* (1830–40)
by an unidentified artist
United States
Silk; 31 x 31¹/₄ in.
Gift of Elizabeth and Eleanor Broadhead,
1980
134970

Masonic apron (1850–75)
by an unidentified artist
United States
Silk, metallic thread, and metal sequins;
15 x 16 in.
Gift of Mrs. Charles Whipple, 1880
2036

55 *Dress* (ca. 1880)
by an unidentified artist
United States
Wool, silk, linen, and cotton; 55 in. (length)
Gift of David O. Ives, 1976
133939

48 *Christening dress and booties* (1847)
by an unidentified artist
Boston, Massachusetts
Cotton; 41 in. (length)
Gift of General Francis Henry Appleton, 1924
117556

18 *Waistcoat front* (late eighteenth century)
by an unidentified artist
Probably France
Silk and linen; 24¹/₄ in. (length)
Gift of Mrs. H. G. Byng, 1950
128074

61 *Evening cape* (1900–1910)
by Liberty and Company
London
Wool and silk; 65 in. (length)
Gift of Mr. and Mrs. S. Morton Vose, 1998
137950

38 *Collar* (1825–35)
by an unidentified artist
New England
Wool and silk; 23³/₄ x 15¹/₄ in.
Gift of Ruth King Richardson, 1947
127197

20 *Moccasins* (late eighteenth or early
nineteenth century)
by an unidentified Native American artist
Northeastern United States
Deerskin, silk, and metal; 4 x 9¹/₂ x 3³/₄ in.
E3712

44 *Tray* (ca. 1840)
by an unidentified Huron artist
Northeastern United States
Birch bark, moose hair, and thread;
8³/₄ x 7³/₄ in.
Gift of Mr. and Mrs. Charles D. Carey, 1990
E77743

Shoes (1855–75)
by an unidentified artist
United States
Wool, silk, and leather; 9¹/₂ x 3 in.
Gift of Alice Dockham, 1937
122969

26 *Sampler* (1803)
by Anne Kimball (1791–1871)
Newburyport, Massachusetts
Silk and linen; 28 x 22 in.
Gift of Timothy A. Ingraham, 2000
138077

66 *The Fishing Lady* (1939)
by Nannie Jenks Borden Phillips (1877–1963)
Topsfield, Massachusetts
Wool, canvas, wood, gilding, and glass;
34¹/₂ x 55 in.
Gift of the estate of Nannie Jenks Borden
Phillips, 1963
130442

2 *Gloves* (1640–60)
by an unidentified artist
England
Leather, silk, linen, metallic thread, and
metal spangles; 12³/₄ x 7 in.
Gift of John Howland, 1822
106845

*Creation of the World, Petit Point 2 from the
Birth Project* (1984)
by Judy Chicago (b. 1939)
1984
United States
Drawing on silk mesh, border designs, and
color specification by Judy Chicago; petit
point in silk by Jean Berens; 10³/₄ x 15 in.
Loaned by the Albuquerque Museum,
New Mexico

Salt Marsh V (1998)
by Linda Behar
United States
Cotton and paint; 3⁷/₈ x 5³/₄ in.
Loaned by Dr. Irving Cooper

A poignant verse, "when this you see remember me," worked on early American needlework demonstrates the ability of embroidery to serve as a link between the past and the present. Since the eighteenth century, embroidery has been used to express ideas about memory through the commemoration of personal or public events, as part of mourning rituals, and as expressions of shared experiences, nostalgia, and historical revivals. Many of these deeply personal works suggest various ways in which the past has informed and influenced the experience of the present. Early nineteenth-century memorial embroideries, such as painted and embroidered silk pictures and samplers, are a significant body of schoolgirl art that commemorates public figures, private individuals, and family members. Also included in this section are embroidered works created to reflect the artist's experience during world events such as the two world wars fought in the twentieth century. Colonial Revival embroideries of the early twentieth century utilize design elements appropriated from the art and decorative arts of the colonial period and adapted to convey messages about cultural identity and values. Works of contemporary art suggest a personal exploration of memory and events in the artist's life or in society.

4 *Sampler* *(ca. 1665)*
by Mary Holingworth (1650/52–94)
Salem or Boston, Massachusetts
Silk and linen; 25 x 7^1/$_2$ in.
Bequest of George Rea Curwen, 1900
4134.39

63 *Sampler (1915)*
by Mary Saltonstall Parker (1856–1920)
Salem, Massachusetts
Cotton and linen; 21^1/$_4$ x 14^1/$_4$ in.
Gift of Mrs. Francis Tuckerman Parker, 1979
134863

64 *Sampler (1918)*
by Mary Saltonstall Parker (1856–1920)
Salem, Massachusetts
Cotton and linen; 20^1/$_4$ x 11^5/$_8$ in.
Gift of Mrs. Francis Tuckerman Parker, 1980
135061

24 *The Parting of Hector and Andromache*
(1800–1810)
by Caroline Williams (1789–1825)
Boston, Massachusetts
Silk, metallic thread, paint, glass, wood, and
gilding; 28^1/$_4$ x 25^1/$_4$ in.
Bequest of Hope Gray in memory of Samuel
S. Gray, 1979
134702

25 *Embroidered and painted memorial (1803)*
by Eliza Passarow (1788–1834)
Boston, Massachusetts
Silk, paint, glass, wood, and gilding;
23^1/$_2$ x 21^3/$_4$ in.
Gift of George P. Messervy, 1904
100272

22 Memorial entitled *Sacred to the Memory*
of the Illustrious George Washington
(early nineteenth century)
by an unidentified artist
Probably Essex County, Massachusetts
Silk, linen, watercolor, and ink; 12 x 11^1/$_2$ in.
Museum purchase, 1928
119451

36 Memorial entitled *Sacred to the*
Memory of Mrs. Eliza Daland (1820)
attributed to Sally Whittredge (b. 1804)
Salem, Massachusetts
Silk, chenille, ink, and watercolor; 22 x 20 in.
Museum purchase with funds donated
anonymously and from American Decorative
Arts acquisition funds, 1999
137967

59 *Dress (ca. 1895)*
by Eliza Philbrick (1836–1927)
Salem, Massachusetts
Wool, linen, brass, and cotton;
56 in. (length)
Gift of Eliza Philbrick, 1919
109674

23 *Memento Mori (ca. 1801)*
by an unidentified artist
Salem, Massachusetts
Silk, ink, pencil, and human hair;
14^3/$_4$ x 12 in.
Gift of Emilie C. Ropes, 1938
123162

Handkerchief (1945)
by Morris Larkin (b. 1922)
United States
Cotton; 16 x 16 in.
Loaned by Mr. and Mrs. Morris Larkin

68 *Blanket: Wrapped in My Parents' Love*
(2000)
by Linda Behar
United States
Cotton and wool; 63 x 93 in.
Museum purchase, 2000
138136

Catalogue Entries

Sampler *(1610–20)*
by Anne Gower (d. 1629)
England
Linen; 17 x 7 in.
Gift of Captain Samuel J. Endicott, 1918
106842

The white-work sampler made by Anne Gower, the earliest example in the museum's collections, holds a distinctive place in the history of American textiles. It is one of a small group of objects to survive from the period of British colonial settlement of America in the seventeenth century that historians call the Great Migration. The maker presumably packed the sampler among her family's belongings when she boarded a ship in England in 1628 and sailed to the New World. It provides compelling evidence about how settlers transported craftsmanship and cultural practices from England to the American colonies.[8]

The intricate needle lace demonstrates Anne Gower's proficiency in advanced needlework techniques that were applied to clothing and fine household linens in England during the early seventeenth century. Threads were carefully drawn out from the ground fabric and then embroidered in intricate floral or geometric patterns creating a delicate lace. Portraits of the Jacobean and Stuart periods often depict garments featuring lace edgings on collars, cuffs, caps, and infant clothing. By learning needle lace and embroidery, girls from affluent families acquired skills that displayed their families' status, education, and social aspirations. In the context of colonial migration, it suggests the sophisticated lifestyle that some settlers left behind when they migrated to the New World.[9]

Anne Gower was the wife of John Endicott (b. ca. 1600 and d. 1665), governor of the Massachusetts Bay Colony. On 20 June 1628, the Endicotts and fifty other settlers sailed from Weymouth, England, on board the *Abigail*. After a voyage of ten weeks, the ship arrived in early September at Naumkeag (the present city of Salem), where they were greeted by Roger Conant and the few surviving members of the Dorchester Company, one of the ill-fated joint stock companies. During the winter, the settlers suffered from the effects of cold weather and inadequate housing, and many succumbed to disease. On 16 February 1629, Anne's cousin Matthew Craddock wrote from England to John Endicott hoping "to hear my good cousin, your wife were perfectly recovered of her health." Anne Gower died a short time after the letter was written.[10]

The sampler remained in the possession of the Endicott family until 1828, when Charles Moses Endicott loaned it to the museum of the East India Marine Society in Salem. It was marked in ink with the museum's catalogue number 3997 that still appears on the front of the sampler. In 1893, the museum exhibited the sampler in the Massachusetts State Building at the World's Columbian Exposition in Chicago, the largest of the nineteenth-century world fairs held in the United States. It was displayed in a case devoted to "Old-time needlework."[11] In 1918, a century after the original loan to the museum, Captain Samuel G. Endicott donated the sampler to the Essex Institute.

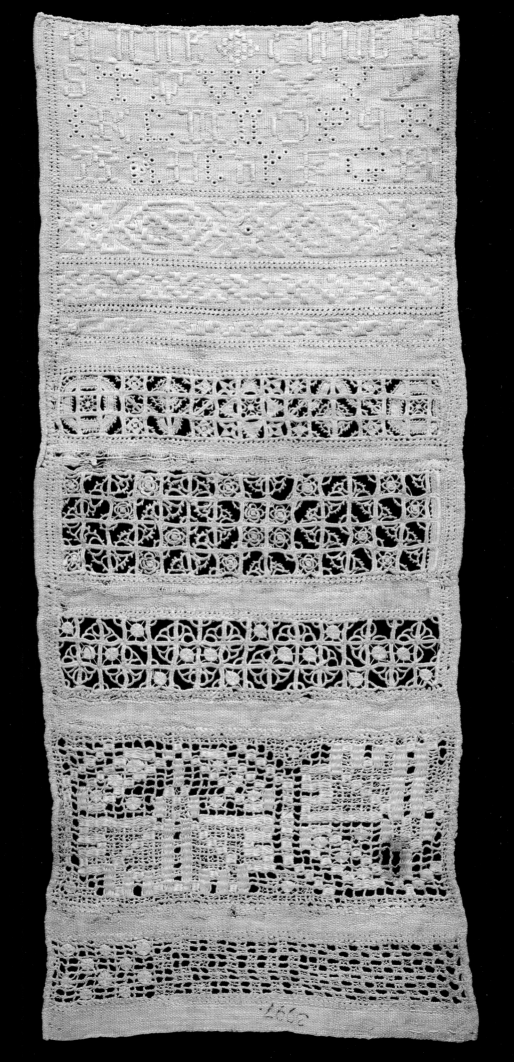

3

Gloves (1640–60)
by an unidentified artist
England
Leather, silk, linen, metallic thread, and metal spangles; 12¾ x 7 in.
Gift of John Howland, 1822
106845

Elaborately embroidered gloves were important ceremonial objects and status symbols in seventeenth-century England and colonial America for both men and women. Gloves were exchanged between monarchs and members of the nobility as symbols of loyalty, given by families at weddings and betrothal ceremonies to seal covenants and agreements, and at funerals as expressions of mourning. Some gloves feature emblems symbolic of specific meanings or purposes. These gloves, which were owned by Governor John Leverett (1616–79) of the Massachusetts Bay Company, feature cuffs ornamented with expensive gold and silver raised embroidery, small spangles, and metallic fringe. They were probably made by a professional embroiderer in London where the retail trade in embroidered clothing and accessories flourished.[12]

Governor Leverett was a prominent merchant and a political and military leader in the Massachusetts Bay Colony. Leverett lived in England between 1655 and 1661 as an agent of the colony at the Court of the Lord Protector. It is likely that Leverett acquired the gloves during this period, although it is possible that objects of this kind were also available as imported goods in Boston. A descendant recorded that Leverett wore the gloves "on public days and on his attendance on the Great and General Court." A portrait of Leverett by an unidentified artist depicts him in military garb wearing a leather jerkin with silver ornamental fasteners, a sword belt, helmet, and gloves with deep gauntlet cuffs.[13] Sumptuary laws in seventeenth-century Massachusetts dictated that clothing be "suitable to the estate or quality of each person." Consquently, gloves such as these would signify that the wearer was a person of importance.[14]

Embroidered cabinet and case (1655–85)
attributed to the daughters of Governor John Leverett
New England or England
Silk, linen, metallic thread, wood, gilding, gesso, and brass; 12 x 10⁷/₈ x 7¹/₂ in.
Gift of Mrs. Justin Whittier, 1925
118284

Embroidered cabinets were among the most complex embroidery projects undertaken by schoolgirls in seventeenth-century England. Having completed polychrome and white-work samplers, some students finished their educations by completing cabinets, frames for looking glasses, or other objects covered in raised embroidery and beadwork. Cabinets functioned as containers for valuables such as jewelry, scent bottles, writing equipment, needlework tools, and miniatures. A number of examples completed by English schoolgirls survive in British and American museums and private collections. The Leverett cabinet may be the most complete surviving example of an embroidered cabinet with colonial American provenance.[15]

Family tradition suggests that one or more of the six daughters of Governor John Leverett was the maker of the cabinet. The girls were born between 1651 and 1673 in the Massachusetts Bay Colony. The Leverett family lived in England between 1655 and 1661 while John Leverett represented the colony at the English court. It is possible that the components for making the cabinet were acquired in England and later brought back to Massachusetts when the family returned home after the completion of the diplomatic mission.[16] Textile scholars believe that panels marked with hand-drawn patterns and materials for constructing cabinets were sold as kits in London and other urban centers. This would account for the uniformity of design and for the repeated use of certain imagery on a number of surviving cabinets.[17]

The scene on the front panels of the cabinet depicts the presentation of Queen Esther that is chronicled in the Bible (Esther 2:5). Depictions of women from Old Testament accounts were popular subjects for needlework because they were appropriate role models and heroines for young women. British textile curator Xanthe Brooke attributes this popularity to Esther's association with persecuted religious and political minorities and to her bravery that inspired women during the tumultuous years surrounding the English Civil Wars. This association may also have been appealing to New England Puritans.[18] It is possible that the sloping panel on the front of the lid showing a scene of a sailing vessel and two figures in a small boat rowing to shore may depict colonial migration or transatlantic travel to New England.[19]

A Leverett descendant, Mrs. Justin Whittier, donated the cabinet to the Essex Institute in 1925. It had been exhibited at the museum fifty years earlier at the *Exhibition of Antique Relics* held as a fund-raising event for the Centennial Exhibition in Philadelphia in 1876, the first world's fair in the United States.[20]

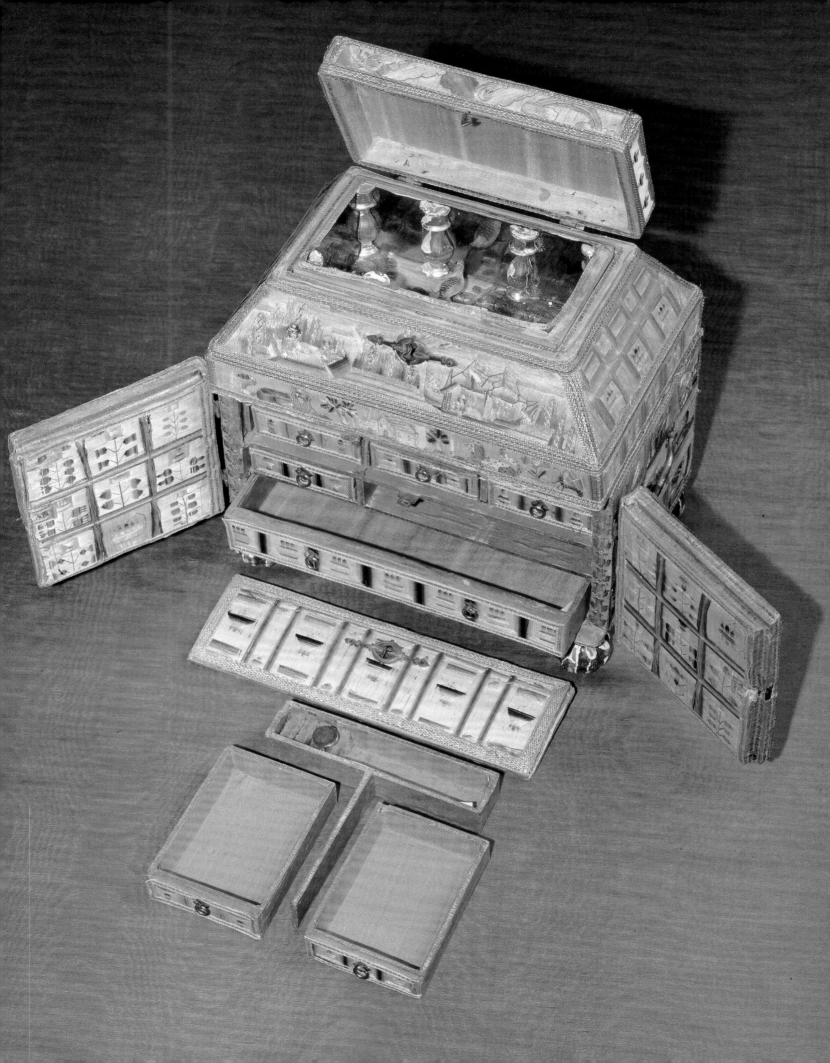

Sampler *(ca. 1665)*
by Mary Holingworth *(1650/52–94)*
Salem or Boston, Massachusetts
Silk and linen; 25 x 7¹/₂ in.
Bequest of George Rea Curwen, 1900
4134.39

Band samplers that feature floral and geometric patterns arranged in horizontal rows are the most common samplers to survive from seventeenth-century England and colonial America. Embroiderers derived the motifs from popular pattern books published in England such as Richard Shorleyker's *A Schole House for the Needle* (1632) or John Boler's *The Needle's Excellency* (1624). They also adapted design elements from emblem books, herbals, botanical works, prints, and book illustrations. The floral motifs reflect the popularity of botany and gardening, and the angular vines show the influence of strap work and knotted devices, patterns that found expression in art, architecture, decorative arts, and garden design of the period. The donor recorded that the square motifs at the top of the sampler were intended for the corners of shawls.[21]

Mary Holingworth was the daughter of merchant and tavern owner William Holingworth and his wife, Elinor Story Holingworth. A family tradition suggests that Mary had been a pupil of a Madame Piedmonte of Boston, a "celebrated instructress of that day." In 1675, Mary Holingworth married Philip English, an immigrant from the Isle of Jersey who became an affluent merchant through international maritime trading in Europe, England, and the West Indies. The family acquired great wealth and owned significant holdings in real estate, vessels, and personal property. In 1692, both Mary and Philip English were accused and imprisoned during the Salem witchcraft trials. Aided by ministers and government officials, the English family escaped to New York, where they remained for two years. Shortly after returning to Salem in 1694, Mary Holingworth died at the age of forty-two.[22]

In 1793, the Reverend William Bentley recorded in his diary the account of Philip and Mary English and their involvement in the witchcraft trials as told to him by their great-granddaughter Susannah Harthorne. He made this note about Mary English: "His Wife had the best education of her times. Wrote with great ease & has left a specimen of her needlework in her infancy or Youth. It is about 2 feet by 9 inches, like a sampler. It concludes with an Alphabet & her name, in the usual form. The figures are diversified with great ease & proportion, & there are all the stitches known to be then in use, & an endless variety of figures in right lines, after no example of nature."[23] George Rea Curwen, a descendant of Philip and Mary English, bequeathed the sampler to the Essex Institute in 1900.

5

Pastoral canvas-work picture (1735–50)
by Sarah Ropes (1717–90)
Salem, Massachusetts
Wool, silk, and linen; 11 x 9 in.
Gift of Charlotte S. Nichols, 1936
133428

Pastoral subjects were among the most prevalent and influential genres of art in eighteenth-century England and colonial America. Country scenes with genteel figures engaged in a variety of rural pursuits found expression in paintings, portraiture, wallpaper, print and book illustrations, textiles, ceramics, and other objects. Artists and craftsmen drew inspiration from a variety of sources including depictions of ancient Greece and Rome, English country estates, landscape paintings by artists such as Claude Lorrain, and Biblical subjects. In the hands of embroiderers, the pastoral landscape became one of the most important groups of needlework produced in colonial America. Often called "fishing lady pictures" after a recurring image of a female angler, these creations were completed by schoolgirls attending a number of Boston-area boarding schools. Needlework historians, including Nancy Graves Cabot, Betty Ring, and others, have identified French and English engravings, prints, and book illustrations that inspired design elements on individual embroideries.[24] It is also possible that simple wood-block illustrations found in almanacs, chapbooks, playing cards, or other ephemera may also have inspired needlework designs.[25]

The small pastoral canvas-work picture made by Sally (Sarah) Ropes is an unusual and appealing example of this genre. It combines a naïve treatment of perspective, scale, and proportion with a sophisticated use of color that enhances the vibrancy of the scene. The bird suspended in mid-air above the picnicking couple and the gestures of the girl fleeing the wolf add an amusing cartoon-like quality. The embroidery technique is tent stitch worked in wool and silk on a linen canvas. The maker used French knots to create the wooly texture of the two large sheep in the foreground and the large red strawberries.

Sally Ropes was the daughter of Salem cordwainer Samuel Ropes and his wife, Lidia Neal. Sally had four siblings, three brothers and one sister. Sally died at the age of seventy-three in 1790 on the same day as her youngest brother, Benjamin. The Reverend William Bentley records the funeral of the siblings in his diary: "A Procession this afternoon attending the burial of two persons, a Mr. Ropes & his sister. They both died in one house, have been long confined, & nearly the same length of time." Sally's embroidered picture descended in her brother's family and hung for many years in the Peirce-Nichols House (a historic structure now owned by the Peabody Essex Museum) at 80 Federal Street in Salem, Massachusetts.[26]

6

Sampler (1750)
by Sarah Erving (1737–1817)
Boston, Massachusetts
Silk and linen; 16¹/₂ x 13 in.
Gift of Mr. and Mrs. Charles Edward Cotting, 1976
M16522

Sarah Erving of Boston, Massachusetts, worked this sampler in 1750 at the age of thirteen. It is one of a group of related samplers from colonial Boston that exhibit similar stylistic characteristics and may have been associated with a school that has yet to be identified. In particular, they feature a distinctive figural motif of two men carrying a large bunch of grapes between them. This motif is derived from the biblical account recorded in Numbers 13 about Caleb and Joshua who were sent as spies to explore the land of Canaan on behalf of Moses and the Israelites. When they returned, they carried with them a single cluster of grapes on a pole as evidence of the abundance of the Promised Land. The museum owns two other samplers with this motif, and other examples reside in museum and private collections. The concept of the Promised Land held great appeal for colonial Americans.[27]

Other motifs demonstrate the longevity of the band-sampler tradition in New England established in the seventeenth century and carried over well into the next century. The geometric floral motifs and angular vines that emulate strap-work patterns are similar to those worked on English and colonial Massachusetts band samplers in the seventeenth century.[28]

Sarah Erving was the daughter of merchant and mariner John Erving and his wife, Abigail Phillips Erving. A nephew later wrote that "My aunt Sarah was as pure a human character as ever existed, but she was so plain in person that grandfather prophesied that she would never get a husband." Despite this prediction, Sarah married Samuel Waldo (1723–70) in 1762 at the Brattle Street Church in Boston. Two years after her marriage, Waldo commissioned the artist John Singleton Copley to paint a portrait of Sarah that is also owned by the Peabody Essex Museum. Although born in Boston and educated at Harvard, Waldo settled his family in Falmouth, near Portland, Maine. The couple had six children, four boys and two girls. Samuel Waldo served as an officer during the French and Indian War and later as a probate judge for Cumberland County. He engaged in land speculation and acquired vast holdings in Maine, Massachusetts, and Connecticut. The Waldo family lost much property following Samuel's death in 1770 and during the American Revolution due to their Loyalist sympathies. Sarah Waldo returned to Boston by 1778 and lived there until her death in 1817. She was buried in the King's Chapel Burying Ground.[29]

13

7

Pastoral canvas-work picture *(ca. 1765)*
by Sarah Chamberlain (1750–96)
Boston or Salem, Massachusetts
Wool, silk, linen, and metallic thread; 8³/₈ x 10 in.
Gift of Mary B. Chamberlain, 1951
128281

The small pastoral needlework made by Sarah Chamberlain depicts a fashionably dressed lady picking fruit in an imaginary landscape accompanied by her dog. The eighteenth-century pastoral tradition in art, literature, and music evoked an idealized vision of the natural world, a glimpse of Arcadia, or an earthly paradise. Gardening and landscape architecture of the time manicured and civilized the physical environment. The human figures that populated that landscape were also idealized and ennobled in harmony with their setting. Rozsika Parker notes that the portrayal of women in eighteenth-century needlework suggests a new feminine ideal—that of the aristocratic lady leading a life of leisure, taste, and suitable social pursuits.[30]

Several visual elements in this picture underscore its meaning as a depiction of an idealized eighteenth-century lady. The clothing worn by the woman is highly fashionable, comparable to that worn in paintings and portraiture of the time. Though strolling outdoors, the lady wears a yellow dress with contrasting blue petticoat and heeled shoes. The bodice of the dress features a stomacher or triangular panel embroidered in metallic thread, a fashionable accessory.[31] The lady is accompanied by her dog, a symbol of fidelity and affection. The dog may be a spaniel, the ownership of which was restricted in England to the aristocracy and therefore in colonial America was symbolic of privilege and status. The most provocative element, however, is the woman's gesture, reaching out to pluck a ripened red fruit from the tree. Fruit and flowers in colonial portraiture have long been associated with women's social and familial roles, symbolizing fertility, productivity, nurture, and the cultivation of character and virtue.[32] The gesture may suggest more than just the simple harvesting of summer's bounty.

The donor of the needlework attributed the piece to Sarah Chamberlain who was born in 1750 and died on 27 April 1796. Very little else has yet been discovered about her.

15

8

Pastoral canvas-work picture (1760–65)
by Anna Ward Mansfield Henfield (1744–1832)
Salem or Boston, Massachusetts
Wool, silk, linen, and paint; 15¼ x 23¾ in.
Gift of Ethel Hammond, 1947
126995

The pastoral scene embroidered by Anna Ward exemplifies the English country house ideal of the mid-eighteenth century. Like other examples of this genre, the work features an elegantly dressed lady and two gentlemen in a verdant landscape with rolling hills, trimmed specimen trees, and two large houses in the Georgian style. The countryside is filled with sheep, hunting dogs, birds, flowers, and large strawberries. The gentleman offers a small basket of berries to the lady, who holds a trained bird on her wrist. The woman's gesture draws emphasis to her fashionable dress. She pulls aside the over-skirt of the dress to reveal a ruffled petticoat and high-heeled shoes. A second man wearing a tricorn hat and red jacket smokes a long-stemmed clay pipe while he rests at the base of the tree.[33]

The facial features and flesh tones on all the figures have been painted in chalky pigment rather than stitched. The sheep and the strawberries are worked in French knots to create a textured effect. The work features its original painted wooden frame and glazing.

Anna Ward was the daughter of Miles Ward Jr. (1704–92) and his wife, Hannah Derby Hathorne Ward (1702–96). Miles Ward Jr. worked in the furniture trade as a joiner. In 1762, Anna married Jonathan Mansfield Jr. (1744–79), a merchant and metalworker whose occupation was listed in 1774 as an anchorsmith. The couple had seven children. Following her first husband's death, Anna married Joseph Henfield in 1780 and had four additional children. The embroidered picture descended through the female line of the Henfield family until it was donated to the Peabody Museum of Salem in 1947. A family notation indicates that Anna Ward Henfield completed other embroidered pictures that may still be in existence.[34]

9

Pastoral canvas-work picture (1750–80)
by an unidentified artist
Salem or Boston, Massachusetts
Wool, silk, and linen; 11⅝ x 14¾ in.
Gift of Mrs. Edward Law, 1941
124819

The female figure resting at the base of a tree is related to the "reclining shepherdess" motif, a popular element of eighteenth-century pastoral canvas-work pictures. Needlework scholars Betty Ring, Nancy Graves Cabot, and others have noted the recurrence of this pattern on embroideries dating from the third quarter of the eighteenth century made in Boston and the surrounding region.[35] The elegant dress of the male and female figures suggests that they are members of the gentry engaged in leisure pursuits on country estates or ornamental farms rather than actual farm laborers. Rozsika Parker notes that the shepherdess and milkmaid in eighteenth-century English and colonial American embroideries embody an ideal of femininity based on an aristocratic standard that transcended class and was indicative of the true nature of women.[36]

One striking visual element is the unnaturally large size of the flowers, especially the red blossom in the foreground, in comparison to the human figures and the buildings on the horizon. This naïveté of design has sometimes caused early American schoolgirl embroideries to be classified as folk art although their historical, aesthetic, and cultural context is more complex than this might imply. The relationship to prevailing artistic styles, the transmission of design sources from one medium to another, and the role of needlework within the formal educational curriculum of women make schoolgirl embroidery and its relationship to folk art a subject worthy of further consideration.

It is not known who made this work, although family tradition records that the piece was owned by Mrs. Nathaniel (Caroline Saunders) Saltonstall (b. 1793) of Salem, Massachusetts. However, it probably dates from an earlier generation of the Saunders or Saltonstall families.[37]

10

Sampler (1764)
by Elizabeth Herbert (1751–67)
Salem, Massachusetts
Silk, metallic thread, and linen; 17¾ x 14½ in.
Gift of Mrs. Percival Foster, 1981
M19027

The superb sampler worked by Elizabeth Herbert when she was twelve years old demonstrates how the English pastoral landscape tradition could be adapted for sampler borders. A well-dressed gentleman seated in the lower left corner has caught a fish at the end of a long rod. Angling was a genteel pastime on English country estates, and it became a convention of portraiture and landscape painting that suggested the cultivated leisure of the aristocratic class.[38] A lady in a silken gown holds a long shepherd's crook and tends a flock of four wooly sheep, an example of the "reclining shepherdess" motif common in the needlework genre known as "fishing lady pictures."[39]

It is not known what school Elizabeth Herbert attended, although a nearly identical sampler completed by classmate Dorothy Ashton (1751–1802) in the same year survives in the collections of the Museum of Fine Arts, Boston.[40] The similarity of the two samplers demonstrates that the creation of the design must be credited to the teacher more than to the individual student. The border is filled with a sense of movement created by the multicolored bands of stitching that zigzag up the sides of the sampler forming receding spatial planes. More than a dozen lively creatures share the rolling countryside, including deer, birds, sheep, a butterfly, and an exotic spotted leopard. The sampler features an extensive use of metallic thread on the radiating sun in the top margin, the scalloped border around the central panel, and clothing details such as the buttons on the man's jacket and waistcoat and the stomacher attached to the bodice of the woman's dress.

Elizabeth Herbert was the fourth of seven children born to Captain Benjamin Herbert (1709–61) and Elizabeth Fowler Herbert (1717–72) of Salem, Massachusetts. Her father was a ship owner and captain who traded in the southern colonies, the Caribbean islands, Spain, and Portugal.[41] Elizabeth died only three years after completing the sampler. Mrs. Mary Vial Holyoke of Salem noted in her diary on 18 April 1767, "Betty Herbert buried."[42]

The sampler's verse suggests a Christian religious interpretation to the shepherding theme.[43]

THE WAKEFUL SHEPHERDS NEAR THIR FLOCKS WERE WATCHFUL FOR THE MORN

BUT BETTER NEWS FROM HEAVEN WAS BROUGHT YOUR SAVIOUR CHRIST IS BORN.

E. Herbert

AWAKE ARISE BEHOLD THOU HAST

THY LIFE A LEAF THY BREATH A BLAST

ELIZABETH HERBERT HER SAMPLER AGED TWELVE 1764

21

11

Valence from a set of bed hangings (ca. 1770)
by the Eveleth family
North Shore of Massachusetts
Wool and linen; 83⅛ x 13 in.
Gift of Mrs. Fannie P. Rust, 1918
107291

Bed furnishings were among the most expensive household items owned by colonial Americans and were symbols of status, affluence, and fashionable taste. In addition to their obvious functional purpose, beds were the largest pieces of furniture in most households and when fully furnished with textiles could make powerful visual statements within the domestic interior. In the eighteenth century, beds were often located in the public rooms on the first floor of the house such as the parlor, although the trend toward moving beds upstairs to second-floor chambers increased over the course of the century. "High beds" with tall posts were arrayed with bed hangings that typically consisted of curtains, valences, a head cloth, tester, bases attached to the bed rail, and sometimes a matching coverlet. Valences were suspended around the tester or canopy that was mounted to the top of the bed posts. Valances were sometimes made in sets of three because the head cloth completed the fourth side when the bed was pushed up against the wall.[44]

Although bed hangings were constructed in a wide variety of silk, woolen, linen, or cotton textiles, those that were embroidered survive in considerable numbers in museum collections. Described in period documents as "workt" or "wrought," the embroidered hangings were often stitched in crewel yarns on a linen ground. Abbott Lowell Cummings in his treatise on bed hangings suggests that respect for "personal effort," as well as the emotional attachment to objects made by family members, may account for the disproportionately high survival rate of embroidered bed hangings.[45]

The design precedents for the floral and arborescent motifs favored on embroidered bed hangings were the "tree of life" pattern derived from palampores and other textiles from India, the English pastoral landscape tradition, and the imaginative interpretation of Chinese landscapes known as "chinoiserie."[46] A dated coverlet stitched by Mary Breed of Boston in 1770 in the collections of the Metropolitan Museum of Art in New York features birds, trees, and floral motifs that are similar to the Eveleth valances. The taste for the blue-and-white color scheme may have been inspired by Chinese ceramics. Blue-and-white crewel embroidery has become a symbol of colonial America due to the popularity of the Colonial Revival textiles produced by the Deerfield Blue and White Society in Deerfield, Massachusetts, in the 1890s.[47]

The donor attributed the valances to Susanna (1607?–59), wife of Silvester Eveleigh or Eveleth (1603/4–88/9) of Essex, Massachusetts. The style and materials, however, suggest a much later date than her lifetime. It is more probable that the maker was one of their descendants, many of whom continued to live in Ipswich, Massachusetts, and other local communities on the North Shore in the eighteenth century.[48]

12

Sampler *(1774)*
by Elizabeth Derby (1762–1814)
Salem, Massachusetts
Silk and linen; 15½ x 10¾ in.
Gift of Louisa Lander, 1894
3543

Worked on the eve of the American Revolution, the undulating floral vine that forms the border of Elizabeth Derby's sampler became a popular element of sampler design in New England for the next fifty years. Delicate floral vines became fashionable as decorative elements in wallpaper, woven and printed textiles, and other decorative arts in the third quarter of the eighteenth century. The richly colored silks of the sampler remain remarkably bright and accentuate the motifs such as the small strawberry plants and basket of flowers below the first alphabet.

The two brief verses of the sampler express values that were held up as models for young women in the eighteenth century. "Idleness is The Root of all Evil" emphasizes the industriousness expected of colonial American women. "Modesty adorns the Fair Sex tho Life" promotes the self-effacing propriety expected of adult women.

Elizabeth Derby was the daughter of Elias Hasket Derby (1739–99) and Elizabeth Crowninshield Derby (1736–99) of Salem, Massachusetts. Her father was the wealthiest merchant and shipowner in Salem during the late eighteenth century. His ships traded internationally in Europe, the West Indies, and the Baltic region, and his ship the *Grand Turk* was among the first American ships to visit China. Elias Hasket Derby is often cited as "the first American millionaire."[49] In 1783, Elizabeth Derby married Captain Nathaniel West (1756–1851) against the wishes of her parents. The couple had six children and maintained an elegantly furnished home in Salem and a country house, Oak Hill, built in 1801 in South Danvers (now Peabody), Massachusetts. The Wests commissioned furnishings from the finest artists and craftsmen in Boston and Salem and purchased goods from abroad. Three of the rooms from Oak Hill survive as period rooms in the Museum of Fine Arts, Boston. The couple divorced in 1806 in bitter trial proceedings that were recounted in local newspapers and diaries. Following the divorce, Elizabeth Derby West was estranged from her family and Salem society. She died in semi-seclusion in 1814 at the age of fifty-two.[50]

13

Table cover (1779)
by Susannah Hiller (1751?–1822)
Salem or Boston, Massachusetts
Silk and linen; 26¹/₂ x 19¹/₂ in.
Bequest of Annie Regina Foster, 1949
127945

Family tradition records that Susannah Hiller embroidered this white linen table cover for her trousseau prior to her marriage in 1779. Its small size may indicate that it was intended for use on a tea table or dressing table. She stitched the patterns in bright yellow silk on a white linen ground that is bound with a fringed tape on all four sides. The design motifs include a delicate floral vine around the perimeter of the cloth with a large medallion-like rose in the center. The rose was the ancient symbol of Venus, the goddess of love. Two large peacocks in full plumage stand on either side of the central motif. In Christian iconography, the peacock sometimes signifies immortality based on an ancient legend that the bird's flesh did not decay. However, the peacock could also symbolize vanity. It is difficult to determine which combination of meanings the maker intended.[51]

Susannah Hiller was the daughter of Boston silversmith Joseph Hiller Sr. (1721–58) and his wife, Hannah Welsh (1720–74). Her father was the nephew of the renowned Boston schoolmistress Mrs. Susanna Hiller Condy (1686–1747), and he may have named his daughter after her.[52] Needlework scholar Betty Ring has credited Mrs. Condy with being "the most likely originator of both the fishing lady pictures and Boston's heraldic embroidery." Mrs. Condy's legacy may have continued after her death through her sister-in-law Abigail Stevens Hiller who advertised a school in Boston that opened in 1748 and continued into the 1750s.[53] Although the influence of these schoolmistresses on Susannah Hiller's work is difficult to assess, it is important to note the family connection and possible exposure to the work of these important figures in early American embroidery.

Susannah Hiller married Nathaniel Foster (b. 1752) of Boston in 1779. The couple had three children: Nancy, Susan, and Henry Gardner Foster. In the 1790s, the family commissioned artist Nathaniel Hancock to paint a group of miniature portraits of Susannah and Nathaniel Foster and their three children; the portraits are now in the collections of the Peabody Essex Museum.[54]

14

Sampler (1778)
by Nabby Mason Peele (1767–1834)
Salem, Massachusetts
Silk and linen; 15$\frac{1}{2}$ x 19 in.
Gift of Mary T. Saunders, 1890
109643

Schoolgirl Nabby [Abigail] Mason Peele attended the school kept by Mistress Sarah Stivours in Salem, Massachusetts. The survival of several samplers marked with the teacher's name has made this the best known of the schools that taught embroidery in eighteenth-century Salem. Sarah Fiske Stivours (1742–1819), the daughter of a Salem clergyman, married Jacob Stivours, a baker from Holland, in 1771. The couple separated after less than one year of marriage, and Mistress Stivours supported herself by running a school for girls that included instruction in embroidery. The stylistic similarity between the samplers worked by students at the Stivours school demonstrates the influence that schoolmistresses had over the work of their pupils in this period.[55] A comparison of the Peele sampler with one worked by Sally Rust (see catalogue entry 17) also owned by the Peabody Essex Museum helps to delineate the characteristics of samplers from the Stivours school.

The border of the sampler features the idealized pastoral landscape that was a popular subject in art, decorative arts, literature, and music in Britain and colonial America during the eighteenth century. A shepherd and shepherdess stand on either side of a tree set in a landscape with sheep. The symmetrical alignment of the figures and tree is similar to Adam and Eve samplers worked in the Boston area in the early eighteenth century but shifted to a more secular context. Large floral sprays fill the borders. Stitched in silk on a linen ground, the sampler features the long surface satin stitch worked in crinkled silk floss, frequently in a diagonal direction, that is a characteristic of embroideries worked in Essex County, Massachusetts.[56]

The verse of the sampler was derived in part from the Reverend Isaac Watt's *Lyric Poems Sacred to Devotion* and expresses thoughts on the Christian religious calling and salvation.

LORD I ADDRESS THY HEAVENLY THRONE

CALL ME A CHILD OF THINE

SEND DOWN THE SPIRIT OF THY SON

TO FORM MY HEART DIVINE.

IN THY FAIR BOOK OF LIFE DIVINE

MY GOD INSCRIBE MY NAME

THERE LET IT FILL SOME HUMBLE PLACE

BENEATH THE SLAUGHTERED LAMB.[57]

Nabby Mason Peele was the daughter of a wealthy mariner and merchant, Jonathan Peele Jr. (1731–1809), and his wife, Margaret Mason Peele (1728–1814). In 1790, Nabby married John Dabney (1752–1819), a bookseller and printer who operated a private circulating library in Salem. The couple had one son and two daughters who lived to adulthood. Widowed at the age of fifty-two, Nabby remained active in church and charitable activities and was a shareholder in the Salem Female School, an influential educational institution for women in the Federal period.[58]

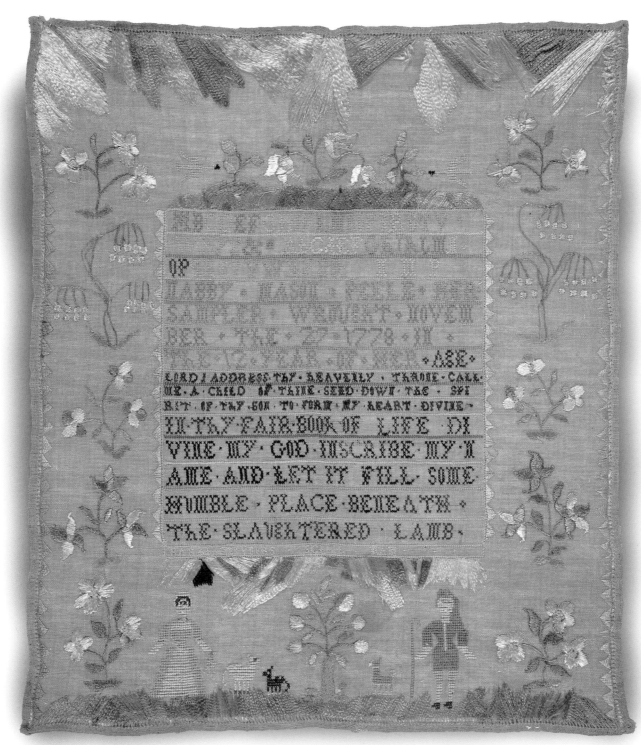

MARY NASH POOLE HER SAMPLER WROUGHT NOVEM BER THE 22 1778 IN THE 12 YEAR OF HER AGE

LORD I ADDRESS THY HEAVENLY THRONE CALL ME A CHILD OF THINE SEND DOWN THE SPI RIT OF THY SON TO FORM MY HEART DIVINE IN THY FAIR BOOK OF LIFE DI VINE MY GOD INSCRIBE MY N AME AND LET IT FILL SOME HUMBLE PLACE BENEATH THE SLAUGHTERED LAMB

A detail of the reverse of the sampler.

15

Sampler *(1783)*
by Mary Richardson *(1772–1824)*
Salem, Massachusetts
Silk and linen; 24$\frac{1}{4}$ x 23$\frac{1}{2}$ in.
Gift of Lucy L. Caller, 1938
123559

Mary Richardson's sampler completed in 1783 is among the finest of surviving examples made in eighteenth-century Salem. The elaborately embroidered border combines elements of the English pastoral landscape tradition with the symmetry and regularity of New England samplers. A lady and gentleman in stylish clothing stand centered at the bottom of the sampler. He has doffed his black tricorn hat in a gesture of salutation or respect. She holds a spray of flowers, perhaps a gift to or from her admirer. They exemplify the courtly couple and capture the ideal of courtship and marriage in the eighteenth century. The trees in the lateral borders expand into an undulating floral vine with oversized roses and carnations that encircle the sampler. An unusual motif is the winged angel head at the top center of the border more commonly associated with gravestone carving.[59]

In the early twentieth century, several authors attributed the Richardson sampler to the school kept by Sarah Stivours in Salem based on the use of the long surface satin stitch worked in crinkled silk floss. Although that technique is recognized as a characteristic of samplers made at schools in Salem and the surrounding region, it appears that the maker attended a school that has yet to be identified. A very similar sampler made by Sally Bott (1772–1826) in 1784 is also in the collections of the Peabody Essex Museum.[60]

Mary Richardson was the daughter of Captain Addison and Mary Greenleaf Richardson of Salem. She was eleven years old when she made the sampler. In 1793 at the age of twenty-one, Mary married Penn Townsend (1772–1846), a master mariner engaged in the international maritime trade with ports in Europe. He was also a privateer during the War of 1812. The couple had four children. Mary died in 1824 at the age of fifty-two.[61]

The sampler verse reads as follows:

Mary Richardson Is My Name and With My

Needle I did The Same and If My Skil Had Been

Better I Would Have Mended Every Letter

This Needle Work Of Mine Can Tell When a

Child Is Learned Well By My Parants I Was

Tought Not To Spend My Time For Nought

This I Did In The 12 Year Of My AGE 1783

16

Embroidered coat of arms of the Fisk family (ca. 1784)
by Lydia Fisk (1768–85)
Boston, Massachusetts
Silk, metallic thread, and metal spangles; 18⅜ x 18⅜ in.
Bequest of the Misses Allen, 1920
112131

The embroidered coats of arms made in Boston were among the most expensive, technically exacting, and illustrious examples of schoolgirl needlework made in eighteenth-century America. Needlework historian Betty Ring has shown that they were created to be "elegant and prestigious household decorations" rather than as hatchments or painted coats of arms used in mourning practices in Europe, Great Britain, and colonial America. Coats of arms were symbols of family identity that conveyed messages about affluence, social standing, gentility, and heritage to people who observed them hanging in private homes. Under the instruction of an accomplished schoolmistress, schoolgirls created the family's coat of arms as the culmination of their formal education.[62]

Betty Ring attributes the coat of arms made by Lydia Fisk to the school operated in Boston by Eleanor Druitt. Mistress Druitt probably used patterns provided by heraldic painters John Gore and his son Samuel who kept a workshop on Queen Street in Boston. The Gores used stencils to transfer the shield and surrounding design to the fabric and then added the crest and emblazonment. These were based on an English book of heraldry or the "Roll of Arms" compiled by the Gores that contained almost one hundred painted coats of arms. The Gore "Roll of Arms" survives in the collections of the New England Historic Genealogical Society in Boston.[63]

Lydia Fisk was the daughter of General John Fisk (1744–97) and his wife, Lydia Phippen (1747–82). Her father was a master mariner, merchant, and extensive property owner in Salem, Massachusetts. He commanded the warship *Tyrannicide* during the American Revolution and after the war was active in the Massachusetts state militia, eventually attaining the rank of major general.[64] Lydia Fisk died from consumption in 1785 at the age of seventeen. The Reverend William Bentley recorded that, prior to her death, a "New Light" minister, a Mr. Hopkins, attempted to "intrude his services" into the Fisk family, particularly focusing on Lydia. Mr. Hopkins was not well received, and Bentley noted that his efforts were "repulsed with generous disdain."[65]

33

17

Sampler (1788)
by Sally Rust (1776–1803)
Salem, Massachusetts
Silk and linen; 21 ¹/₄ x 20 ¹/₂ in.
Museum purchase with funds donated anonymously, 1995
137741

The sampler worked by Sally Rust in 1788 is a second example in the museum's collections from the school kept by Mistress Sarah Stivours in eighteenth-century Salem. Although the format is similar to the sampler worked by Nabby Mason Peele ten years earlier, there are notable differences between the two samplers. The male and female figures on this sampler are more boldly rendered in the long surface stitch rather than the meticulous cross-stitch used on the Peele sampler. The pastoral landscape is populated with a wider variety of animals and birds, including spotted black and white sheep. The upper border of the sampler features an additional motif, a floral arbor that encloses a basket of flowers. A large bird perches at the top of the arbor. Patches of the long surface satin stitch worked in a diagonal direction suggest an abstracted depiction of the blue sky and the green grass at the top and bottom margins of the sampler.[66]

The verse on the sampler emphasizes the value of education, the guidance of older adults, and productivity. It is one of the common verses worked on New England samplers in the eighteenth century and asserts the object's ability to convey the accomplishment of its maker.[67]

SALLY RUST

HER SAMPLER WROUGHT 1788 IN THE 13

YEAR OF HER AGE.

THIS NEEDLE WORK OF MINE CAN TELL

WHEN I A CHILD WAS LEARNED WELL

AND BY MY ELDERS I WAS TAUGHT

NOT TO SPEND MY TIME FOR NOUGHT

SARAH STIVOUS SCHOOL MADAM 12

Sally Rust was the tenth of sixteen children born to Henry Rust (1737–1812) and his first wife, Lydia Janes Rust (1740–1808). Her father was a cabinetmaker and merchant. In 1801, Sally married John Deland (Daland) of Salem as his second wife. The museum owns a silver pitcher made by silversmith Joseph Foster (1760–1839) of Boston for Sally Rust Daland around the time of her marriage. The couple had one child, a son, before her death in 1803 at the age of twenty-seven.[68]

18

Waistcoat front (late eighteenth century)
by an unidentified artist
Probably France
Silk and linen; 24¼ in. (length)
Gift of Mrs. H. G. Byng, 1950
128074

The suit of an eighteenth-century gentleman consisted of a jacket or coat, a waistcoat, knee-length breeches, silk stockings, and buckled leather shoes. By the second quarter of the eighteenth century, the cut of the jacket revealed the waistcoat to a greater degree, and the waistcoat became increasingly ornamental. Constructed of rich fabrics and embellished with embroidery, metallic braid, trim, and fancy buttons, the waistcoat could match or stand in contrast to the color and materials of the suit. Professional embroiderers in France and England fabricated component parts of embroidered waistcoats and suits as export items to the American colonies and other parts of the world. Americans could purchase the embroidered components and then have them made to size by local tailors.[69]

This waistcoat front features exquisite colored embroidery worked in satin stitch and chenille on an ivory satin ground fabric. The floral embroidery along the front opening is characteristic of the naturalistic flowers associated with the rococo style. Less common are scenes of landscapes or figures such as the cockfighting motif worked on this vest. Americans have practiced cockfighting as a spectator sport and gambling event since the seventeenth century. Historians have noted that cockfighting in early America was "principally a masculine pastime" and was particularly popular in the plantation society of the southern colonies. The donor noted that the waistcoat belonged to a member of the Lawrence family who wore it at a reception for George Washington. Several American presidents, including Washington, attended cockfights on a regular basis.[70]

19

Embroidered coat of arms of the Peirce family (1797)
by Sarah Peirce (1780–1835)
Salem, Massachusetts
Silk, metallic thread, and metal spangles; 17⅜ x 17⅜ in.
Gift of the estate of Charlotte Sanders Nichols, 1935
FIC1688

In September of 1797, Benjamin Peirce (1776–1831) wrote from Harvard College in Cambridge to his sister Sarah (Sally) Peirce to commend her on the completion of her embroidered coat of arms. He commented on the embroidery: "George gives me . . . a very flattering account of your Arms. However, making allowance for his partiality, I don't hesitate to set them down for beautiful. I congratulate you on your being set at liberty."[71] The letter captures the familial pride and sense of accomplishment that a young woman and her relatives must have felt at the completion of these large and complex embroideries. Worked in richly colored silk, gold and silver metallic thread, and metal spangles on an ivory silk ground, the coat of arms features raised embroidery on the scrollwork and other details in the emblazonment.[72] The extensive use of metallic thread would have made the large embroidery shimmer with reflected light while it hung in the Peirce family home. The wood-framed mansion house designed by architect Samuel McIntire for Sally's father, merchant Jerathmiel Peirce (1747–1827), still stands at 80 Federal Street in Salem and is owned by the Peabody Essex Museum.[73]

As a young child, Sally Peirce attended the school kept by schoolmaster Nathaniel Rogers and his wife, Abigail Dodge Rogers (1764–1817), in Salem. Sally's name appears in the account book kept by Rogers in 1792 and 1793, and it seems likely she worked a simple marking sampler dated 1792 while attending their school.[74] A reward of merit documents that Sally's sister Eliza Peirce also attended the school.[75] Betty Ring attributed the Peirce coat of arms to the school kept by Eleanor Druitt (active between 1771 and 1799) in Boston because of stylistic similarity to other examples from that school.[76] Although admittedly similar to examples from the Druitt school, the Benjamin Peirce letter introduces a possible connection to the school of Mrs. Rogers of Salem.

The Rogers school has been the subject of much speculation by scholars because contemporary diarists record that the school was noted for exceptionally fine needlework. The Reverend William Bentley once compared the needlework from the school of Mrs. Rogers to the academy kept by Judith Saunders (1772–1841) who with Clementina Beach operated one of the premier female academies in Federal-period New England. Yet, no documented examples of ornamental embroidery from the Rogers school have been firmly identified.[77]

Having taught in Salem since 1789, Nathaniel Rogers was dismissed in December of 1796 as school-master of the town grammar school. It appears that Abigail continued to teach female students into 1797. In Benjamin Peirce's September 1797 letter to Sally, following his compliments on her coat of arms, he continued in this manner: "I feel myself much hurt on hearing of Mrs. Rogers' intention of moving out of town—however I hope it will turn out only 'talk.' He may go, if he pleases; provided he'll only leave her." While the letter is not conclusive, it suggests a possibility that Sarah continued her association with Mrs. Rogers's school until shortly before its closing in the fall of 1797. By November of 1797, Mr. and Mrs. Rogers advertised in the newspaper that they proposed opening a school in Newburyport. It lasted but a short time and by the spring of 1799, Mrs. Rogers reopened a school in Salem that continued in operation until 1816.[78] A controversy about the curriculum at Mrs. Abigail Rogers's school began to brew in 1800 that involved opposing views about women's roles in society and female education and that set the Peirce and other Salem families in turmoil (see the case study by Elysa Engelman beginning on page 141).

Sally Peirce married her first cousin George Nichols, a sea captain and merchant, in 1801, and the couple had nine children. Their marriage took place in the east parlor of the Peirce-Nichols House that had been remodeled by Samuel McIntire in the Adamesque style for the occasion. Sally's wedding dress survives in the museum's collections.[79]

20

Moccasins *(late eighteenth or early nineteenth century)*
by an unidentified Native American artist
Northeastern United States
Deerskin, silk, and metal; 4 x 9¹⁄₂ x 3³⁄₄ in.
E3712

Native Americans have traditionally utilized a variety of embroidery and related techniques to ornament garments, leather, and other materials. As Europeans migrated to North America and encountered the indigenous people already living there, a highly complex interchange of cultural ideas and practices commenced that continues to the present day. A melding of beliefs and practices can be seen in art and functional objects shared by both cultures.[80]

Moccasins were an article of Native American clothing adopted by European settlers for use as practical everyday footwear or as decorative indoor slippers. Both European and Native Americans of the late eighteenth and early nineteenth centuries had traditions of ornamented footwear that combined functional and aesthetic purposes.[81] Huron and other Native American artists in the northeastern United States and Canada produced embroidered moccasins for sale to travelers and European settlers at trade centers and tourist destinations. Some moccasins were similar in style to those made by Native American people for their own use, but others were adapted from European forms and ornamentation to make them appeal to consumer tastes. The buckled strap and pleated green silk edging are concessions to European footwear fashions. Ruth Phillips notes that moccasins made for trade with Europeans sometimes "omit the ankle cuffs and add silk ribbon appliqué and new styles of floral decoration." The delicate floral spray intricately embroidered on the toes of moccasins gives evidence of this type of artistic and cultural interchange.[82]

21

Sampler *(ca. 1800)*
by Sally Martin Bowen (1789–1872)
Marblehead, Massachusetts
Silk and linen; 20$^{1}/_{8}$ x 16$^{1}/_{4}$ in.
Gift of Frederick W. Story Sr., 1981
135370

Sally Martin Bowen's sampler is a fine example of the distinctive samplers worked in Marblehead, Massachusetts, a community on the North Shore of Massachusetts supported by seafaring enterprises, both mercantile trade and fishing, in the eighteenth and nineteenth centuries. The green linen ground fabric became popular in the late eighteenth century in coastal New England. It provided a vibrant background for the pastel shades of silk used to compose the floral and landscape elements. The eighteenth-century pastoral landscape tradition remained influential in the early nineteenth century. The lower border of the sampler evokes this earlier style. The technique used to render the grass— vertical rows of pale blue cross-stitch interspersed with long stalks in stem stitch—give a soft textured quality to the ground. Other elements, such as the urns with flowers, reflect the taste for the neoclassical style that dominated art and decorative arts in early nineteenth-century America.

Needlework historian Betty Ring has attributed a group of related samplers to the school run by Martha Tarr Hanover Barber (1734/35–1812) from the 1780s through the first decade of the nineteenth century and continued by her daughter Miriam Barber through the 1820s. It is likely that Sally Bowen attended the school. Her father, Nathan Bowen (1752–1837), helped with the administration of Martha Barber's estate following her death in 1812. It is assumed that Sally worked the sampler around 1800, although the date was removed from the inscription at the center of the sampler sometime after its completion. In April of 1813, Sally Bowen married Isaac Story Jr., and the couple eventually had at least twelve children.[83]

The sampler verse is from a hymn by the Reverend Isaac Watts:

On Earth let My example shine

And when I leave this state

May heaven receive this soul of

Mine to bliss divinely great.[84]

ABCDEFGHIJKLM
NOPQRSTVWX
YZ

Sally
M. Bowen
her sampler
worked in the
year

On Earth let my example shine
and when I leave this state
may heaven receive this soul of
mine to bliss divinely great

22

Memorial entitled *"Sacred to the Memory*
of the Illustrious George Washington" *(early nineteenth century)*
by an unidentified artist
Probably Essex County, Massachusetts
Silk, linen, watercolor, and ink; 12 x 11 1/2 in.
Museum purchase, 1928
119451

The death of George Washington (1732–99) at his Virginia home, Mount Vernon, in December of 1799 profoundly affected the citizens of the new nation. Having served during the French and Indian Wars and later as the commander in chief of the Continental Army during the American Revolution (1775–83) and the first president of the newly formed United States of America (1788–96), Washington was the most renowned public figure in the country, and his achievements had been celebrated in prints and engravings during the latter years of his lifetime. Following his death, he gained a mythic status that continues to the present day and was made a symbol of republican virtues and the principles on which the nation was founded. Washington was immortalized in prints, engravings, textiles, mourning jewelry, and other objects, and became a subject of numerous schoolgirl embroideries.[85]

Many of the memorial embroideries were adapted from prints or engravings of similar subjects and used mourning imagery in the neoclassical style. Curator Wendy Wick has noted that the imagery combines elements of mourning art, European allegorical traditions, and resurrection and apotheosis themes.[86] In this memorial, the female allegorical figure of Columbia is seated at the base of a memorial plinth and obelisk reading a copy of the Constitution of the United States. The obelisk is inscribed "Pater Patriae" (father of the country) encircled by an oval wreath. Inscribed on the plinth is the following text: "Sacred to the Memory of the Illustrious George Washington, who was born Feb. 22, 1732. Ob. Dec. 14, 1799." A poem of homage appears on the base of the plinth but is partially obscured by the leather-bound book. A weeping tree frames the scene on the left side. The needlework may once have had a reverse-painted glass mat that no longer exists. The maker of the memorial is unknown, but needlework historians Davida Deutsch and Betty Ring have attributed the embroidery to Essex County, Massachusetts, based on similarities to other memorials worked in the region.[87]

23

Memento Mori *(ca. 1801)*
by an unidentified artist
Salem, Massachusetts
Silk, ink, pencil, and human hair; 14¾ x 12 in.
Gift of Emilie C. Ropes, 1938
123162

Among the most unusual memorial embroideries in the museum collections is this work in memory of Elizabeth Carlton, who died in 1801. It is an example of print work done in black silk on a white silk ground in imitation of engravings or other print sources of the early Federal period. The tiny stitches that fill in a number of the motifs are meant to emulate stipple engraving.[88] The memorial uses a variety of common symbolic elements in the neoclassical style, such as the obelisk on a plinth, the funerary urn, the weeping trees, and the laurel wreaths. Its most unusual attribute, however, is the use of long strands of brown human hair, possibly that of the deceased, to fill in the background of the urn. Although locks of hair had long been a treasured keepsake of a deceased loved one, and human hair was often incorporated into lockets and other forms of jewelry, using human hair as embroidery floss was less common. The act of stitching with human hair from a loved one must surely have increased the highly personal nature of the work. Two other similar works survive in the museum's textile collections, suggesting that a local school that has yet to be identified taught this type of embroidery.

The inscription on the work is as follows:

Memento Mori.

Tho' Man is Mortal, God is Just.

Sacred to the Memory of Elizabeth Carlton

Who died Decr. 26. 1801.

Aged 39.

Salem

Heav'n gives us friends to bless the present Scene,

Resumes them to prepare us for the next.

All evils natural are mortal Goods;

All Discipline Indulgence on the whole.

Elizabeth Carlton (1762–1801) was the daughter of Deacon Samuel Holman (1736–1825) and his wife, Reith (1735?–1801). Her father was a ruling elder in the North Church of Salem. In 1787, she married Benjamin Carlton, and the couple had five children before her death in 1801.[89]

24

The Parting of Hector and Andromache (1800–1810)
by Caroline Williams (1789–1825)
Boston, Massachusetts
Silk, metallic thread, paint, glass, wood, and gilding; 28¼ x 25¼ in.
Bequest of Hope Gray in memory of Samuel S. Gray, 1979
134702

Sarah Anna Emery of Newburyport, Massachusetts, recalled seeing in the early years of the nineteenth century a painted and embroidered picture that depicted the parting of Hector and Andromache. She described it in this fashion: "The couple were presented in a final embrace on the portico of a palace. Massive pillars supported the roof; the floor was of alternative squares of black and white, representing marble. A little apart stood the nurse bearing the infant heir in her arms, while the background showed a plain dotted by tents."[90]

The subject is derived from an episode in book six of Homer's epic poem *The Iliad*. The scene depicts Hector, eldest son of the king of Troy, as he takes leave of his wife, Andromache, and infant son to return to the battlefield. The moment is one of great drama and pathos as Hector was later killed in battle, Andromache enslaved by an Achaean captor, and their son murdered. Art historian Rozsika Parker has noted that the appeal of this classical tale for early nineteenth-century women was in its expression of loss, separation, and renunciation.[91] The design of the needlework was adapted from an engraving by James Watson after a painting by Angelika Kauffmann published by Robert Sayer in London in 1772.[92] Kauffmann (1741–1807) was arguably the most successful woman artist of her time and enjoyed enormous popularity in America through reproductions of her paintings in engravings. Americans received Kauffmann's work with enthusiasm, both for its portrayal of women that manifested ideal femininity and for her own merit as a role model for young women.[93]

Caroline Williams of Newburyport, Massachusetts, worked this embroidered picture while attending the Berry Street Academy in Boston that was run by schoolmaster William Payne (1746–1812). It is embroidered in silk and metallic thread on a silk ground with painted details. Schoolteachers sometimes employed artists or decorative painters to do the painting to enhance the artistic quality of the needlework. It features its original reverse-painted glass mat and gilded wooden frame.[94]

Caroline Williams Fecit.   Berry Street Academy.

THE PARTING of HECTOR and ANDROMACHE.

25

Embroidered and painted memorial (1803)
by Eliza Passarow (1788–1834)
Boston, Massachusetts
Silk, paint, glass, wood, and gilding; 23¹/₂ x 21³/₄ in.
Gift of George P. Messervy, 1904
100272

Following the death of George Washington in 1799, memorial or mourning pictures of public figures and private individuals became a popular subject of schoolgirl embroidery. Memorials appealed to Americans as symbols of refinement and classical virtue as well as expressions of grief. Design sources were usually engravings that schoolgirls or their teachers adapted as patterns for needlework. These engravings were in the neoclassical style that emulated the art, architecture, and decorative arts of ancient Greece and Rome. Neoclassical elements intermingle with Christian iconography and biblical texts.[95] The overall format of the obelisk, urn, and weeping figures is similar to a memorial to Alexander Hamilton and George Washington that inspired a number of schoolgirl embroideries.[96] The angel pointing heavenward appears in a number of print sources and needlework, although its position— seemingly impaled on the top of the obelisk—is awkward. Made of silk embroidery on a silk ground, the picture features a painted sky, facial features, and other details. It is in its original frame and reverse-painted glass mat inscribed "Done by Eliza Passarow 1803."

Eliza Passarow was the daughter of Jacob Passarow, a German immigrant and Boston glass manufacturer who died in 1801 at the age of 35. She was fifteen years old when she embroidered this picture, probably at a school in Boston. It is possible that she appears as one of the female mourners in neoclassical dress on either side of the urn and obelisk. The inscription on the urn is "Jacob Passarow Obt. Aust. 23rd 1801 AE. 35 years. The sweet Remembrance of the Just shall Flourish When he Sleeps in Dust." A biblical quote from Revelation (14:13) appears in the oval on the plinth: "I Heard a voice from Heaven say Blessed are those that Die in the Lord."

26

Sampler *(1803)*
by Anne Kimball (1791–1871)
Newburyport, Massachusetts
Silk and linen; 28 x 22 in.
Gift of Timothy A. Ingraham, 2000
138077

Newburyport, Massachusetts, situated at the juncture of the Merrimack River and the Atlantic Ocean, was a thriving port supported by an inland agricultural region in the eighteenth and early nineteenth centuries.[97] Noted for its architecture, Newburyport is also known for distinctive regional samplers. Most notable are the "shady bower" samplers named after the verse that begins "In this green and shady bower." These samplers feature elaborate landscapes with figures that are unusual interpretations of the English pastoral landscape tradition. Another group of samplers portrays landscapes with fruit trees, birds, animals, and blue or blue-and-white vases filled with flowers.[98] Anne Kimball's sampler worked in 1803 is a fine example of this second type. It displays borders of an undulating floral vine on three sides. The wide lower border depicts a landscape with black and white sheep, a tree with red fruit, and two blue-and-white urns filled with blossoms. Small details such as a strawberry plant, a butterfly, and the two birds in the tree add visual richness to the scene.

The verse of the sampler expresses ideas about industry, religious devotion, and the effective employment of women's time in reading, sewing, and writing.

How blest the Maid whom circling years improve

Her God the object of her warmest love

Whose useful hour's successive as they glide

The book, the needle and the pen divide

Anne Kimball born June 14 1791 wrought this Sampler in The twelfth year of her age Newbury Port 1803

Anne Kimball was the daughter of Captain Edmund Kimball (1762–1847) and Anna Porter Kimball (1762–96) of Wenham and Newburyport, Massachusetts. Her father was a soldier in the American Revolution and later a sea captain and prosperous merchant. In April of 1818, Anne married Dr. Ebenezer Alden (1788–1881) of Randolph, Massachusetts. The couple had six children. Dr. Alden was a physician, author, genealogist, and local historian.[99]

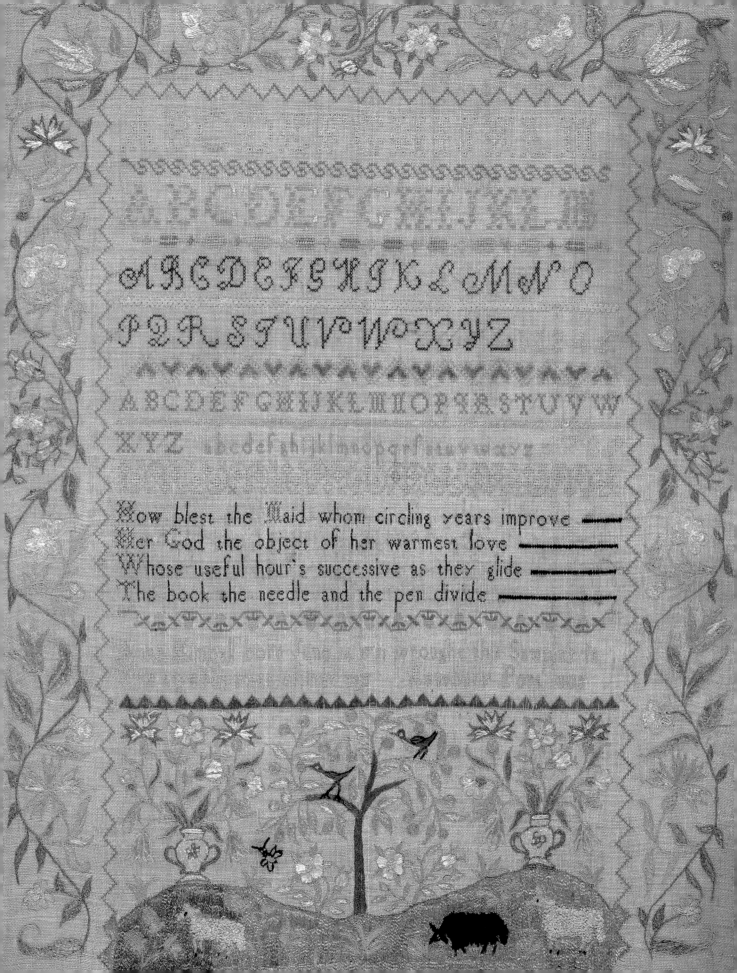

ABCDEFGHIJKLM

$\mathcal{ABCDEFGHIJKLMNO}$

$\mathcal{PQRSTUVWXYZ}$

ABCDEFGHIJKLMNOPQRSTUVW

XYZ abcdefghijklmnopqrstuvwxyz

How blest the Maid whom circling years improve ———
Her God the object of her warmest love ————
Whose useful hour's successive as they glide ————
The book the needle and the pen divide ————

27

Painted and embroidered allegorical picture (1804)
by Maria Crowninshield (bap. 1789–1870)
Dorchester, Massachusetts
Silk, watercolor, metallic thread, and reverse painting on glass; 24³/₄ x 19¹/₄ in.
Gift of Mr. and Mrs. Francis B. Lothrop, 1980
M18627

In August of 1804, Maria Crowninshield at the age of fifteen years wrote a letter from the Ladies' Academy, Clifton Hill, in Dorchester, Massachusetts, to her sister Hannah at home in Salem in which she described the school as "this delightful mansion of happiness."[100] Maria attended the academy run by Mrs. Judith Saunders and Miss Clementina Beach that was renowned for the painted and embroidered pictures based on popular engravings and prints that were created by its students. Like other works from the school, an inscription on the reverse-painted glass mat identifies both the maker and the name of the school: "Wrought by Maria Crowninshield, At Mrs. Saunders & Miss Beach's Academy Dorchester."[101]

The subject of the embroidery is an allegorical scene about female education in the early nineteenth century. It depicts a schoolmistress instructing a pupil in an architectural setting that suggests a temple of learning. Objects such as the globe, lyre, a floral embroidery, artwork, and a piano or harpsichord reinforce the symbolism of education and cultural refinement. A classical goddess rewards the pair with a floral wreath. The book that the teacher and student are studying is *Strictures on the Modern System of Female Education* by the English educational reformer Hannah More. A hotly contested debate over the role of women and female education erupted in England and the United States around 1800. Books by More and other reformers such as the feminist Mary Wollstonecraft were widely read by Americans and polarized opinions on women, social structures, politics, and a number of related issues. (See the case study by Elysa Engelman beginning on page 141.) Hannah More's positions may have appealed to the more conservative mercantile families of Salem and as such may have been deemed an appropriate subject for a schoolgirl embroidery.[102]

Maria Crowninshield was the daughter of Benjamin (1758–1836) Crowninshield and his wife, Mary Lambert. In 1814, Maria married her cousin Captain John Crowninshield (1774–1842) at the home of her grandmother, now known as the Crowninshield-Bentley House, owned by the Peabody Essex Museum. A boarder in the house, the Reverend William Bentley, recorded in his diary that "Much is expected from this match by all parties." The couple had three daughters and two sons.[103]

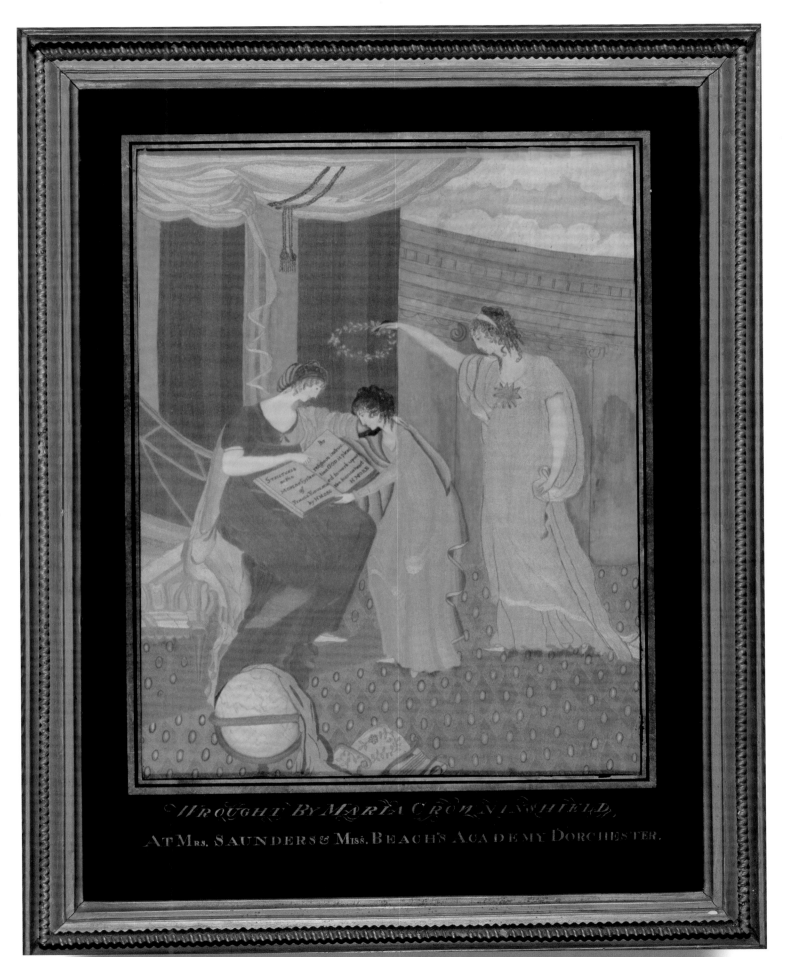

WROUGHT BY MARIA CROWNINSHIELD,

AT MRS. SAUNDERS & MISS BEACH'S ACADEMY DORCHESTER.

28

Sampler *(1806)*
by Elizabeth Briggs *(1796–1866)*
Salem, Massachusetts
Silk and linen; 24⅝ x 23¼ in.
Gift of Elizabeth Wheatland, 1897
3846 (109716)

The large sampler worked in 1806 by Elizabeth Briggs at ten years of age demonstrates the influence of the neoclassical style on schoolgirl needlework after 1800. The large, fluted, two-handled urn based on classical precedents is the dominant motif in the lower border. The undulating floral vine that fills the lateral borders terminates at the top with symmetrically arranged birds on either side of a large floral ornament. The entire border is worked in surface satin stitch using crinkled silk floss that completely covers the linen ground, a characteristic of Essex County, Massachusetts, samplers carried over from the eighteenth century. The sampler survives in its original gilded wooden frame.[104]

Born in Scituate, Massachusetts, in 1796, Elizabeth was the daughter of Elijah Briggs (1762–1838) and Hannah Buffington Briggs (1767–1847). Her father was a shipbuilder in Scituate and later in Salem, Massachusetts. In 1822, at the age of thirty-six, Elizabeth married Richard Wheatland, a mariner, and the couple had three children.[105]

The inscription on the sampler expresses the maker's thankfulness for education and parental guidance and her hope that these will reward her with refinement and moral improvement later in life:

Next Unto God Dear Parents I Address

Myself to You in Humble Thankfulness

For All Your Care And Pains on me Bestow'd

And Means of Learning Unto Me Allow'd.

Go on I Pray And Let me Still Pursue

Those Golden Paths the Vulger Never Knew.

Elizabeth Briggs is my Name And With my

Hand I Have Wrought the Same in the 10th year

Of my age Salem February 15th 1806.

29

Cymbeline (ca. 1807)
by Mehitable Neal (1786–1856)
Dorchester, Massachusetts
Silk, paint, glass, wood, and gilding; 17 x 22^1/$_2$ in.
Museum purchase with funds donated anonymously, 1997
137797

The school kept by Mrs. Judith Foster Saunders and Miss Clementina Beach in Dorchester, Massachusetts, produced some of the most elaborate embroideries made in the Boston area during the early nineteenth century. Founded in 1803, they operated a school for day and boarding students in Dorchester and later in Boston and continued teaching into the 1830s. Their curriculum included general subjects such as reading, writing, English grammar, arithmetic, and plain sewing and also more specialized topics such as French, painting, the use of globes, hair work on ivory, dancing, and embroidery.

Painted and embroidered silk pictures from the school often feature original gilt wood frames with reverse-painted glass mats made by the framer John Doggett of Roxbury. This embroidery is almost certainly one of three framed by Doggett for "Miss Mehitable Neall" on 11 September and 3 October 1807 at a combined cost of $17.50.[106]

The scene is from Shakespeare's play *Cymbeline* and depicts Cymbeline, king of Britain, enraged at his daughter Imogen who married a poor nobleman against his wishes. The king orders the young man to depart from the palace, and Imogen defies her father and clings to her husband as they prepare to leave. The image may have appealed to young women in the early nineteenth century because it embodied changing ideas about marriage based on romantic love rather than the older system of marriages arranged by parents to enhance family status, wealth, and social distinction. The design source of the embroidery was a print engraved by Thomas Burke after a painting by William Hamilton that was published in London by John and Josiah Boydell in 1795. Prints of Shakespeare and other literary and theatrical subjects were very popular as sources of design for embroidery in the early nineteenth century.[107]

Mehitable Neal was the daughter of merchant Jonathan Neal and his wife, Mehitable Eden (1760–86). In 1833, she married Amos Choate (1775–1844) who was the registrar of deeds for Essex County, Massachusetts.[108]

30

Sampler (1807)
by Sarah Todd (b. 1798)
Northeastern Massachusetts or New Hampshire
Silk and linen; 26 x 25^1/$_2$ in.
Gift of Philip T. Andrews, 1977
133922

The large sampler worked by Sarah Todd in 1807 is impressive in its size and in the bold execution of the design. The rose-like flowers and large leaves with scalloped edges that appear in the central basket are neatly coordinated with similar motifs that form the undulating floral border pattern. A large bird dominates the floral spray at the top center of the sampler.

Although the sampler was attributed to Salem, Massachusetts, in the museum's catalogue records, no documentary evidence has yet been discovered that links the sampler's form or maker to that locale. A number of attributes show similarity to samplers produced in the region along the Merrimack River Valley in northern Essex County, Massachusetts, and northward into New Hampshire. The most prominent group is the "bird and basket" samplers of the region surrounding Canterbury, New Hampshire. Betty Ring has documented certain motifs and design elements from this geographic region, such as the "leafy green plumes" and the low, flat basket with scalloped or diapered patterns. However, the sampler lacks the black outlines that are associated with samplers made in Canterbury. The forerunners of the Canterbury motifs seem to be derived from sampler patterns worked in communities in northern Essex County, Massachusetts, such as Ipswich or Newburyport. The patterns may have been transported to the north with a schoolmistress such as Hannah Wise Rogers (b. 1719) of Ipswich, Massachusetts, whose daughters and granddaughters later taught in Canterbury, New Hampshire, or members of the Foster family of Andover and Ipswich, Massachusetts, who settled in Canterbury.[109]

The verse on the sampler expresses a prevalent belief that industriousness was an antidote to sin and inappropriate behavior:

We stand expos'd to every sin

While idle and without employ

But business holds our passions in

An keeps out all unlawful joy

Sarah Todd Born February 28 1798 Wrought This Work AD 1807.

Little is known about the maker of the sampler. She may be the Sarah Todd who was the daughter of Jonathan Todd (1752–1801) and Sarah Todd (1755–1838). She was baptized in 1800 in Rowley, Massachusetts, and married Captain John Howland (1800–1835) of Boston in 1821.[110]

ABCDEFGHIJKLMNOPQ
RSTVWXYZ&

ABCDEFGHIJKLMN
OPQRSTUVWXYZ&

ABCDEFGHIJKLMNOPQRSTUVWXY

abcdefghijklmnopqrstuvwxyz

We stand expos'd to every sin
While idle and without emploz
But business holds our Passions in
And bars out all unlawful joy
Sarah Todd Born February 28 1799 Wrought
This Work A 1807 123456789

61

Embroidered picture *(1800–1810)*
by Maria Chever (1789–1868)
Probably Salem, Massachusetts
Silk, reverse painting on glass, wood, and gilding; 20½ x 17½ in.
Gift of the estate of Sarah A. Chever, 1908
101801

The study of botany and horticulture and the interest in gardening influenced the creation and popularity of floral embroidery in eighteenth-century England and America.[111] Plants were so popular as the subject for needlework that "to flower" became synonymous with embroidery in the mid-eighteenth century. Drawing both from nature and from drawing books became part of the curriculum of young women attending academies that included ornamental accomplishments. Drawing was an essential skill used to transfer patterns to textiles for embroidery.[112] Embroiderers aspired to capture naturalism and botanical accuracy in their needlework, and this required a subtle sense of coloration, shading, and precise stitching. The bouquet features a rose, hyacinth, and tulip tied together with a blue ribbon. Lingering elements of the rococo style are evident in the asymmetry of the composition, the curvilinear quality of the design, and the knotted bow. The work retains its original gilded wood frame and reverse-painted glass mat characteristic of the Federal style.

The maker, Maria Chever, was the daughter of Captain James Chever (1752–1839) and Sarah Brown Chever (1760–1837) of Salem, Massachusetts. She was one of ten children. Her father was a master mariner who traded in the West Indies and Europe. He served on a privateer vessel during the American Revolution and was later appointed an officer at the Salem customhouse during the administration of President Thomas Jefferson. A family reminiscence records that Maria was courted by General Miller, the collector of the port of Salem, and that "he was refused by her." She remained unmarried and lived at the end of her life in Melrose, Massachusetts, with her niece Sarah Ann Chever, a collector and antiquarian.[113]

32

The Dance *(ca. 1815)*
by Frances Leverett
Boston or the North Shore of Massachusetts
Silk, watercolor, and chenille; 17 x 23 in.
Gift of the estate of Clifton Winsor White
in memory of his mother, Sarah Shays White, 1960
129212

Frances Leverett selected a scene of dancing figures in the rural English countryside as the subject of her large painted and embroidered picture. Derived from Oliver Goldsmith's poem "The Deserted Village" written in 1770, the scene depicts contented tenant farmers and villagers frolicking in the open air prior to being evicted from their homes by an unscrupulous landlord. The poem decries the massive changes in land ownership and usage in Great Britain during the eighteenth century and its effects on rural ways of life. The scene captures the happy moment:

While many a pastime circled in the shade,

The young contending as the old survey'd

And many a gambol frolick'd o'er the ground,

And flights of art and feats of strength went round.[114]

The poem and other works by Oliver Goldsmith were popular with American readers in the eighteenth and early nineteenth centuries and would have been suitable for a young female readership. Engravings and book illustrations of literary works inspired the design of embroideries and other related art and decorative arts in the eighteenth and nineteenth centuries. For example, the museum also owns a copperplate printed textile (1790–1800) that is printed with a nearly identical image.[115]

Teachers sometimes hired artists to do the painted details on these embroidered pictures. However, the simple rendering of the faces and other painted details suggest that the painting on this piece may have been completed by the schoolgirl under her teacher's instruction. The use of chenille gives texture and a dimensional quality to the embroidery.

Frances Leverett was the daughter of William Leverett (1770–1811) and Charlotte Whiting Leverett (b. 1775) of Roxbury, Massachusetts. In 1817, she married John Shays of Danvers, Massachusetts.[116]

33

Cornelia and the Gracchi (1808)
by Lydia Very (1792–1867)
Salem, Massachusetts
Silk, paint, and metallic thread; 17$\frac{1}{2}$ x 22$\frac{3}{4}$ in.
Gift of the estate of Lydia L. A. Very, 1906
100507

Lydia Very worked this painted and embroidered silk picture at the "Young Ladies Academy" kept by Mrs. Elizabeth Palmer Peabody in Salem, Massachusetts, between 1808 and 1821. Mrs. Peabody was the mother of the renowned "Peabody Sisters of Salem" and ran a school that taught ornamental needlework and other subjects to augment her family's financial situation.[117]

A clipping glued to the dust cover of the embroidery recounts the tale of Cornelia. "Cornelia the daughter of the Great Scipio and wife of the consul Sempronius, was one day in company with some Roman ladies, who were shewing their trinkets and admiring their jewels, and whose minds seemed wholly occupied about their dress; observing Cornelia sit silent among them, they ask to shew them her jewels upon which with a true maternal pleasure she called her children to her and presenting them to the company of ladies said; 'these are my ornaments; these are my jewels whom I have endeavoured to educate to the good and glory of their country.'"[118]

Cornelia became an important symbol of republican motherhood in the United States during the early nineteenth century and became a role model for young women. A stipple engraving by Francesco Bartolozzi after a painting by the artist Angelika Kauffmann published in London in 1788 was the likely source of the design for this embroidery. Several similar embroidered pictures of this subject survive in museum and public collections.[119]

Lydia Very was the daughter of shipmaster and merchant Samuel Very and his wife, Hannah Putney Very. In 1813, Lydia married her cousin Jones Very (1790–1824) who was also a shipmaster. The couple had six children, four of whom lived to adulthood. Each of their children became distinguished in the field of education and literature. An article in the *Boston Globe* in 1903 about the Very children, "Salem's Famous Family," noted that "Their mother was also well educated and well known in her time as a woman of noble traits. It was under the influence of these high-minded Christian parents that the children were reared."[120]

34

Windsor stools with needlework upholstery (1810–30)
by an unidentified artist
New England
Painted pine, wool, silk, linen, and brass; 15 in.
Museum purchase, Fendelman Collection, 1993
137665.2AB

This pair of Windsor stools is unusual both for their form and for the survival of their original needlepoint upholstery. The stools feature bamboo-turned legs with painted finish. Small workshops in New England, New York, and Pennsylvania made large quantities of Windsor furniture, especially chairs, in the early decades of the nineteenth century. Much rarer than footstools, these medium-high stools functioned as footrests and seating.[121]

The petit point seats feature a reclining stag and leopard surrounded by a floral wreath. Animal motifs, both familiar and exotic, were popular designs for folk art. While the design source is not known, it may have been derived from a woodcut or other popular illustration. These images were easily transferable to a variety of media. Similar motifs appear on hooked rugs, stoneware crocks, wall murals, and other folk art. The original green wool fringe attached with a row of brass tacks completes the upholstered seat.[122]

35

Worktable (1820–21)
painted decoration by Mary L. Poor (1806–84)
North Shore of Massachusetts
Maple, birch, paint, and brass; 29 x 19$^1/_2$ x 15 in.
Museum purchase, 1982
135590

Worktables, or sewing tables, are among the earliest furniture forms made exclusively for use by women. The drawers contained sewing and embroidery implements, and some tables were fitted with a cloth bag suspended from the bottom drawer to store needlework projects. Between 1810 and 1825, painting on worktables and boxes became part of the art curriculum at academies for young women. Sarah Anna Emery of Newburyport, Massachusetts, recorded that "At each of the female schools, in addition to knitting and plain sewing, ornamental needlework was taught, and in some, instruction was given in drawing in India ink and painting in watercolors. . . . Miss Mary Ann Coleman was a good teacher of water color painting; the fruit and flower pieces executed at her school were natural and well done. She also taught painting on wood; several work-boxes and work-stands, painted under her instruction, are still to be seen in the residences of some of our older citizens."[123]

The scenes on the tables were adapted from print sources, engravings, and drawing books.[124] The table painted by Mary L. Poor features small emblems in the neoclassical style that are symbolic of music and love. The top and side panels have British landscape scenes including a castle and Kirstal Abbey. The maker inscribed her name and the date on the front of a drawer: "Mary L. Poor 1821."[125] There are also two inscriptions in pencil on the underside of a drawer: "Still, still for me is every joy awake / of fortune and of friends" and "you know tis true / Well I must Paint away / or Shant Finish Today." A number of similar examples made on the North Shore of Massachusetts survive in private and institutional collections.[126]

Mary L. Poor was the daughter of Enoch and Sarah Poor of Danvers, Massachusetts. In 1824, she married Fitch Pool Jr. (1803–73) also of Danvers, Massachusetts. Her husband was a state representative for Danvers in 1841 and 1842 and also served as librarian of the Peabody Institute. The couple had nine children; their daughter Elizabeth (b. 1839) was the mother of American impressionist artist Frank Weston Benson (1862–1951).[127]

36

Memorial entitled *Sacred to the Memory of Mrs. Eliza Daland* (1820)
attributed to Sally Whittredge (1804–83)
Salem, Massachusetts
Silk, chenille, ink, and watercolor; 22 x 20 in.
Museum purchase with funds donated anonymously
and from American Decorative Arts acquisition funds, 1999
137967

Although this painted and embroidered memorial uses symbolic imagery and mourning conventions that had been popular for twenty years, the quality of the painting and design, the shading of the silk embroidery, and the extensive use of chenille floss make this an unusually fine example of its type. It also demonstrates the longevity of the neoclassical style that continued in fashion over the first three decades of the nineteenth century.

The work commemorates the life of Mrs. Eliza (Elizabeth Whittredge) Daland (1797–1820) of Salem, Massachusetts, who died in 1820 at the age of twenty-two. Eliza was the eldest of five children of merchant Thomas Whittredge (1766–1829) and his wife, Sarah Waters Whittredge (1767–1848). In childhood, Eliza attended the Salem Female School headed by Thomas Cole, and her name appears on a manuscript "List of Scholars" for the years between 1807 and 1810.[128] Historian Joseph B. Felt made the following comment about the school: "So superior was the furniture of its building, and of so high an order were its studies that it was the subject of general conversation and by some, who regarded it as too aristocratic, it was called "The Girl's College."[129] A sampler survives that Eliza worked at age ten, and it records the birth dates of her parents and siblings along with two long verses. An embroidered picture of a vase of flowers completed when she was thirteen may have been worked while she attended the Salem Female School.[130] In 1818, Eliza Whittredge married John Tucker Daland (1795–1858) an aspiring young merchant engaged in the East India trade.[131] Their only child, a daughter named Elizabeth Tucker Daland, was born later that year in December of 1818. Only two years later, at the age of twenty-two, Eliza Whittredge Daland died from hydrocephalus.[132]

The poem printed in the oval on the plinth below the urn records the grief of Eliza's family and suggests a clue to the maker of the embroidery:

Sacred to the Memory of Mrs. Eliza Daland who obit April 22 Aged 22 years

Adieu sister, thy toils and pains are o'er

Though laid to sleep upon thy native shore

Soft by thy slumbers in thy silent grave

Till Christ shall bid the earth give up its dead.

What can forbid thy parents' tears to flow

And smooth this journey down this vale of woe

What can console their long afflicted heart

And resignation to their souls impart

1820

The opening phrase to the poem, "Adieu sister," may be a reference to Eliza's younger sister, Sally (Sarah) Whittredge (b. 1804), who also attended the Salem Female School between 1816 and 1821.[133] As the only female sibling of the deceased, it is likely that she was the maker of the embroidery. It is also possible that she appears in the picture as the adult female mourner wearing the black mourning sash and holds the hand of her niece, Elizabeth, then a toddler. Their beautifully rendered faces may be the work of a professional artist or a skilled amateur.

Sampler (1822)
by Sarah Prescott (1813–1909)
Westford (Forge Village), Massachusetts
Silk and linen; 12³/₈ x 12¹/₄ in.
Gift of the estate of Grace Lawrence, 1936
122669

The sampler worked in 1822 by Sarah Prescott of Forge Village, now Westford, Massachusetts, demonstrates the longevity of the pastoral landscape as a tradition favored in New England sampler making. Symmetrical trees surround a grapevine bearing five large clusters of grapes suggesting the abundance of the countryside. An undulating floral vine surrounds three sides of the sampler with rose-like flowers carefully stitched in tiny French knots.

The verse is an acrostic on the word "virtue." The poem both defines and promotes the advantages of cultivating virtue. It demonstrates the role of verses, mottoes, or phrases on samplers as means of reinforcing religious and cultural values through the contemplation of their meanings while stitching.

Acrostic

Virtue thou source of lasting joy

Inspire our minds our thoughts employ

Reason and experiance show

That virtue makes our bliss below

Unfolds those charms that ne'er decay

Explores true Peace and Points the way

Wrought by Sarah Prescott 1822

Sarah Prescott was the youngest daughter of Abram (1769–1866) and Olive Adams Prescott (1780–1860). Her father was a prosperous farmer, a representative to the general court of Massachusetts, and a deacon of the First Church. Her mother was a weaver who regularly won prizes at regional agricultural fairs between 1824 and 1839. Olive Prescott produced a variety of patterned household textiles including coverlets, blankets, tablecloths, towels, and handkerchiefs in wool, linen, and cotton. Sarah embroidered two white woolen blankets woven by her mother with large floral designs based on the traditional compass-rose pattern. Other textiles embroidered by Sarah and her sisters survive in the museum's collections and in the Fletcher Library in Westford, Massachusetts. These textiles document how embroidery and sewing skills learned by sampler making were used for functional and ornamental purposes in young adulthood. Sarah attended Miss Parker's Academy in Boston in 1828. In 1853, at the age of forty, Sarah married David Lawrence, and the couple lived in Lowell for the remainder of their lives. Their daughter Grace Lawrence donated more than one hundred objects that had belonged to the Prescott family to the Essex Institute in the first three decades of the twentieth century.[134]

38

Collar (1825–35)
by an unidentified artist
New England
Wool and silk; 23³/₄ x 15¹/₄ in.
Gift of Ruth King Richardson, 1947
127197

Collars such as this were clothing accessories worn over the wide necklines of women's dresses in the second quarter of the nineteenth century. Influenced by Romanticism, fashionable women's garments of this period featured wide necklines, full sleeves, narrow waistlines, and full skirts often with elaborate surface ornamentation. Collars, cuffs, purses, and other accessories were frequently embellished with embroidery, lace, and other textile arts. These techniques satisfied the taste for extravagant ornamentation and rendered garments personal and unique to the wearer.[135] Made of soft, white wool and lined with white silk, this collar features an undulating vine of grapes worked in chenille floss. The texture of the chenille contrasts with the flat wool ground and gives the appearance of being embroidered with velvet. Curly wool fringe finishes the edges of the collar, and white silk ribbon ties fastened the collar in place. According to the Victorian "language of flowers," grapes signified charity, mirth, and rural felicity, fitting virtues for a stylish young woman.[136]

39

Apron (1830–40)
by an unidentified artist
United States
Silk; 31 x 31¼ in.
Gift of Elizabeth and Eleanor Broadhead, 1980
134970

This purple silk apron features extraordinary floral embroidery worked in several techniques including chenille embroidery, ribbon work, and crepe work. Chenille embroidery is done using a fuzzy silk thread that derived its name from the French word for caterpillar. Ribbon work employed silk ribbon, often in shaded colors, that was folded and embroidered to create flowers. Crepe work featured strips of sheer silk crepe that were folded and stitched to create blossoms in low relief. All three techniques were taught at Moravian schools in Pennsylvania and North Carolina in the early nineteenth century, and work of this kind is generally attributed to these schools.[137] However, some needlework publications, such as Miss Lambert's *The Hand-Book of Needlework* published in New York in 1842, recorded descriptions of the three techniques.[138] This suggests that these types of embroidery could also have been practiced elsewhere in the United States.

The floral borders contain over a dozen varieties of flowers. It is likely that these carefully rendered blossoms have an association with the "language of flowers," a popular convention in nineteenth-century America. Meanings and sentiments were assigned to individual flowers to create a "coded language of love." For example, the moss rose meant "superior merit" or "pleasure without alloy."[139] In combination, these floral elements could be combined to create complex visual statements or messages usually with romantic implications.

In the eighteenth and nineteenth centuries, the apron became more than a protective garment and functioned as an ornamental accessory worn by affluent women for social ceremonies and events at home. Embroidery and other forms of textile decoration elevated some aprons from utilitarian objects to works of art.[140]

40

Sailor's pants (1830–50)
by an unidentified artist on a voyage from New England to the Pacific Ocean
Wool, cotton, linen, and wood; length: 42 in.; waist: 32^1/$_2$ in.
Gift of Sarah V. G. Peck, 1954
128941

The donor of these unusual embroidered pants recorded that a sailor made them on a voyage from Rhode Island to the Pacific Ocean. They are made of several colored wools and striped cotton ticking. Sailors' crafts such as scrimshaw, wood carving, macramé, and shell work were all shipboard activities that used available materials to fill the long hours and create gifts for loved ones and objects for personal use. Sailors used sewing skills to repair sails and mend clothes and other shipboard textiles. Some sailors who were proficient with the needle employed embroidery to ornament garments, sea bags, and accessories with motifs and symbols important in a sailor's life. Uniforms for seamen were not consistently regulated until the nineteenth century, and sailors were often expected to provide their own clothing. They sometimes embroidered uniforms or other garments that were to be used on shore leave.[141]

The pants are constructed of coarse utilitarian fabrics, probably reused bedding—woolen blankets and striped cotton ticking. The embroidery is running stitch, worked in bold abstract patterns of palm leaves, flowers, stars, and human forms. It is possible that the motifs emulate tattoo patterns practiced by the indigenous people of the South Pacific region that the sailor observed while traveling.[142] European and American sailors adopted tattooing as a form of personal adornment and symbolic expression in the late eighteenth century following the voyages of Captain Cook through the South Pacific. It became a cultural practice associated with sailors and soldiers throughout the nineteenth and twentieth centuries.

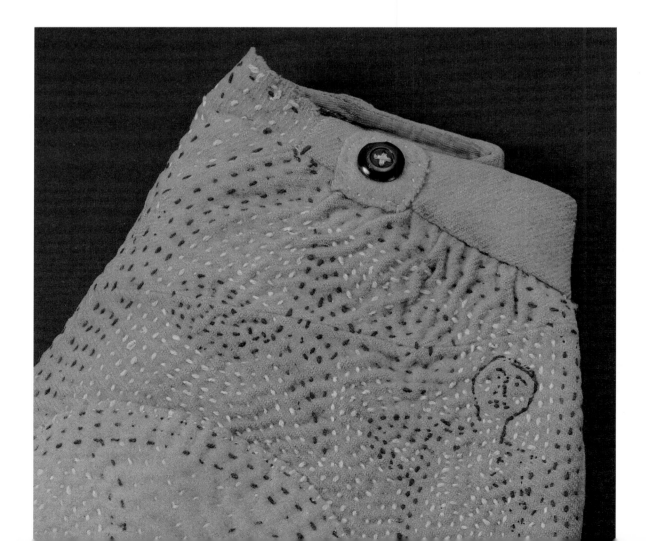

41

Sewing table (ca. 1835)
by an unidentified artist or artists
China
Lacquer on wood, ivory, and silk; 28⁷⁄₈ x 24 x 16³⁄₈ in.
Gift of Mr. and Mrs. Francis B. Lothrop, 1970
E82997

A woman's sewing table was a prized possession in nineteenth-century American homes, and few would rival this example made in China for export to the United States. Constructed of black and gold lacquer on wood, the interior is fitted with numerous compartments to house carved ivory needlework and sewing tools. Many of the original carved ivory tools survive, including a winding clamp, thread reels, and spools. This sewing table was part of a suite of lacquer furniture that also included a *bonheur-du-jour* (cabinet on stand), three sets of nesting tables, a large round center table, and boxes for various purposes.[143]

The black and gold lacquer features scenes of Macau, an island located offshore from the port city of Canton, China, the center of international trade in the eighteenth and nineteenth centuries. On the interior of the lid is a remarkable view of the Praya Grande in a highly detailed rendering that is comparable to Chinese export paintings of the same subject. Chinese landscape scenes and floral motifs cover the remaining lacquered surfaces. All of the pieces of furniture in the suite are marked with a script *W* in a circle for the family of William Shepard Wetmore (1801–62) of New York and Newport, Rhode Island. Wetmore began his career in the China trade as a supercargo on ships owned by his uncles Samuel and Willard Wright of Carrington and Company of Providence, Rhode Island. He conducted business profitably in Canton between 1833 and 1847, when he returned to Newport and built Chateau-sur-Mer, one of the great mansion houses.[144] In 1837, William Wetmore married his first cousin Esther Wetmore of New York who died shortly after the birth of an infant daughter the following year. His second wife was Anstice Rogers (b. 1823) of Salem, Massachusetts, whom he married in 1841. The couple had three children.[145]

42

Embroidered ship portrait or "woolie" (*mid-nineteenth century*)
by an unidentified artist
United States, probably New England
Cotton, silk, and canvas; 17½ x 23¾ in.
Gift of Mrs. Henry Vaughan, 1945
M5706

Woolies are embroidered ship portraits, one of a number of handicrafts practiced by seamen to pass the long hours on sea voyages. Trained in sewing and other textile skills needed to repair sails and mend nets or clothing, some sailors applied these techniques as a recreational activity that produced aesthetic objects for their own use or to be given away as gifts. Although shipowners and captains often commissioned ship portraits from professional artists who specialized in this genre, sailors probably created their own sketches applied directly to the textiles available on board the ships on which they were posted. Yarns and canvas were also easily purchased at ports. Scrimshaw, model-building, knot-tying, and macramé are among the best known of the sailors' crafts, but in recent years, woolies have gained increasing recognition and appreciation among maritime and folk art collectors.[146]

This woolie depicts an unidentified three-masted sailing vessel that flies the American flag and a homecoming pennant. Under full sail, the ship approaches a fort that also flies an American flag and seems to emphasize an American context. While many of the surviving woolies seem to be the product of British seamen, a few examples such as this suggest that American sailors also practiced the craft. The setting may demonstrate the significance of homecoming to sailors who were away on voyages for months or even years.[147]

The donor of the embroidered ship portrait, Mrs. Henry (Elizabeth "Elise" Russell Tyson) Vaughan (1871–1949) of South Berwick, Maine, was a noted twentieth-century collector who specialized in folk art and dolls.[148]

43

Packet of silk thread *(ca. 1840)*
stamped "Linhing"
China
Paper and silk; 25 x 15 in.
Gift of the Massachusetts Society of Colonial Dames of America, 1980
E82207

The paper wrapper on the sample packet unfolds to reveal rainbow hues of silk thread like an artist's palette. Stamped "Linhing," the name of a Chinese merchant, the packet contains eighty-one skeins of silk floss. Embroidery silks, like bolts of fabric, were among the staple exports during the China trade. This packet was exported from China to Boston in 1840 on board the American brig *John Gilpin* of Boston. From there, it was exported to South America. The *John Gilpin* shipping logbook records trading stops on the coast of South America in 1840 and 1841. In addition to textiles, the ship carried furniture, tobacco, nails, lumber, tea, and other items as cargo. Anna Cutler of Boston acquired the packet from her grandfather who served as the supercargo or officer in charge of mercantile transactions on board the *John Gilpin*.[149]

The packet survives in remarkable condition, and the unused silk floss still seems to embody the potential for artistic creation from another time.

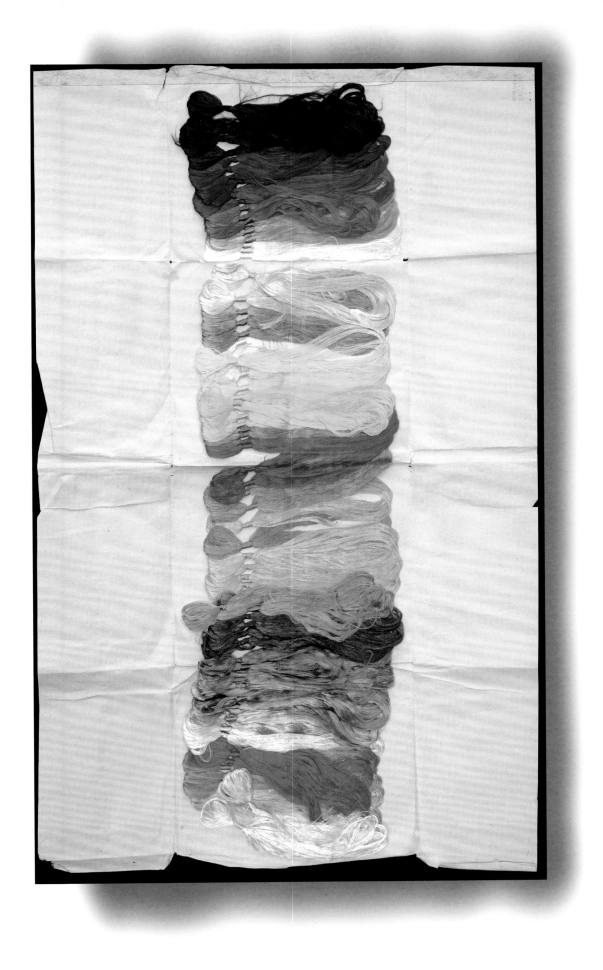

44

Tray *(ca. 1840)*
by an unidentified Huron artist
Northeastern United States
Birch bark, moose hair, and thread; 8¾ x 7¾ in.
Gift of Mr. and Mrs. Charles D. Carey, 1990
E77743

This tray, probably intended for receiving calling cards, demonstrates the intermingling of Native American and European embroidery traditions. Completed in the second quarter of the nineteenth century, the tray was made by an unknown Huron artist who adapted materials and techniques of Native American traditions with design elements of European origin. It is probable that the tray was made as a souvenir or trade item and sold at a tourist site such as Niagara Falls.

The design of the embroidery features Native American men and women walking in a landscape filled with birds and animals. Ruth Philips notes that this depiction is a blending of European idealized views of nature and the Indians' belief in living "in a balanced way on the land, supported by its resources."[150] A large animal dominates the center panel of the tray while the human figures and plants are arranged around the edges.

In the seventeenth and eighteenth centuries, convents in Canada were established to convert and educate young Native American women, and here they were also taught European embroidery techniques. Their birch bark products were sold as a source of revenue. The use of moose hair dyed various colors is characteristic of Huron and other Native American artists working in the northeastern United States and may have been used by Euro-Americans when supplies of embroidery materials were scarce. In the nineteenth century, moose-hair-embroidered objects such as calling card cases, boxes, and wall pockets were popular with the tourist trade.[151]

45

Table cover and table (ca. 1840)
by Mary Berry True (1788–1858) *and Joseph True* (1785–1873)
Wool, cotton, and mahogany; 30³⁄₄ x 28¹⁄₂ in.
Salem, Massachusetts
Gift of Mrs. Arthur T. Wellman, 1974
133540; 133541

The tilt-top table and original needlepoint table cover made by a married couple are a rare survival of collaborative craftsmanship from the first half of the nineteenth century. The table cover bears the initials of Mary Berry True and the date 1840. The table is attributed to Salem woodcarver and cabinetmaker Joseph True and presumably was made for the family's own use. The museum acquired both pieces from the couple's great-great-granddaughter in 1974.

The two objects demonstrate the variety of design influences and stylistic sources prevalent in New England homes in the second quarter of the nineteenth century. In its symmetry, the table cover alludes to the neoclassical taste for center medallions and wreaths. However, the floral bouquet is associated with romanticism, the love of nature, and the picturesque.[152] Several pieces of furniture that have been attributed to Joseph True exemplify the transition from the neoclassicism of the Federal period to the more eclectic styles of the Victorian period. True may have drawn inspiration from English cabinetmakers' pattern books such as Thomas King's *Modern Style of Cabinet Work Exemplified* (1829) that combined "Grecian, Roman, and Gothic Ornaments."[153] The size and form of the table suggest a multipurpose use. It could be set up as a parlor center table, a tea table, or for reading. Its tilting top made it convenient to store when not in use.

Born in Chichester, New Hampshire, Joseph True settled in Salem by the time of his marriage to Mary (Polly) Berry in 1809. Joseph True kept a workshop at 34 Mill Street, and the family resided nearby on High Street. A manuscript account book kept by True between 1810 and 1858 has provided furniture historians with important documentation about the cabinetmaking system in nineteenth-century Salem and the collaboration between specialized craftsmen in furniture production. True was particularly noted for woodcarving, and one contemporary maintained that True's work rivaled that of Samuel McIntire.[154] The couple had four children, three daughters and one son. Following Mary's death in 1858, Joseph lived with two daughters who ran a bonnet shop in the family's High Street house. Following their deaths in the 1860s, Joseph True moved west to Peoria, Illinois, where he lived with his son's family until his death in 1873. The donor recorded that True's descendants in Illinois continued to use the table and its cover until the 1930s.[155]

46

Embroidered dog portrait (1840–60)
by an unidentified artist
United States
Wool, silk, cotton, linen, and glass; 26 x 25 in.
Gift of an anonymous donor, 1919
109449

The emphasis on domesticity as an antidote to the social upheaval caused by industrialization caused a shift in attitude towards pets in the nineteenth century. Once valued for their economic and functional contributions to household and property management, domestic animals and pets increasingly became the objects of sentiment and emotional relationships within American households.[156] One manifestation of these changing views was the popularity of animals and pets as subjects for art and the decorative arts. Among the most admired proponents of this genre was the British artist Sir Edwin Henry Landseer (1802–73) noted for painted canine portraits of pets owned by members of the royal family and the aristocracy. Adaptations of Landseer's and other artists' work were available to Americans through prints and book illustrations. Embroidery designs adapted from animal and pet portraits covered footstools, slippers, cushion covers, and occasionally became the subject of needlework pictures.[157]

The brown-and-white spaniel is worked in a raised plush stitch that has been carefully trimmed to create the contours of the dog's body. The technique for raised embroidery is described in Miss Lambert's *The Hand-Book of Needlework* (1842), and she notes the use of a special tool called a mesh that helped to form the loop of the stitch and cut it when completed. With the stitching complete, the embroiderer combed the fibers to fluff them and then meticulously sheared the plush to give the effect of low sculptural relief. The realistic appearance of the dog is enhanced by the use of glass eyes.[158] A colorful border of small paisley motifs surrounds the picturesque landscape in which the spaniel rests. Unfortunately, the identity of the accomplished maker of this animal portrait is not known.

47

Fire screen (1845–60)
by Mary Hodges (Cleveland) Allen (1817–73)
Salem, Massachusetts
Wool, silk, and mahogany; 59 x 24 in.
Bequest of Marion C. and Elizabeth C. Allen, 1913
103712

Fire screens or pole screens were ornamental parlor furnishings in the nineteenth century. Originally used to shield occupants from the intense heat of the fireplace, fire screens assumed a more decorative and less functional purpose.[159] The large flat screens were well suited for embroidered panels such as the one worked by Mary Hodges Allen. It depicts one of the children of Queen Victoria riding a pony while accompanied by a servant in Scottish dress. Scenes and images of the British royal family's summer home, Balmoral Castle in Scotland, held tremendous appeal for nineteenth-century romantic sensibilities.[160]

The Berlin wool-work embroidery was probably stitched using a canvas stretched over the dark wool ground fabric. The design was stitched through both layers and when completed, the loosely woven canvas could be cut away and removed leaving the embroidery on the plain woolen ground fabric. The technique allowed counted needlepoint to be worked on a finely woven fabric.[161]

Mary Hodges Allen was the daughter of George Cleveland (1781–1840) and Elizabeth Hodges (1789–1834). She married John Fiske Allen (1807–76) in 1842 as his second wife, and the couple had four children, two of whom lived to adulthood. John Fiske Allen was a noted horticulturalist who grew exotic plants such as the night-blooming *Cereus* and the *Victoria regia* water lily at the family's home at 31 Chestnut Street in Salem.[162]

48

Christening dress and booties (1847)
by an unidentified artist
Boston, Massachusetts
Cotton; 41 in. (length)
Gift of General Francis Henry Appleton, 1924
117556

In the eighteenth and nineteenth centuries, white-work embroidery embodied some of the most intricate artistry and craftsmanship created by embroiderers. Without color to engage or distract the eye, the virtuosity of the design and stitching techniques were readily apparent. White work reached a peak of popularity in the nineteenth century when women utilized it to ornament garments, undergarments, and the many fashionable accessories such as handkerchiefs, caps, collars, sleeves, and cuffs required to complete elaborate ensembles. Women also lavished white-work techniques on infant garments such as baby caps, christening dresses, bibs, and other items for the layette as expressions of maternal love and family identity.

The white dress or robe worn for christening symbolizes the purity and forgiveness of sins transmitted to the infant through the ceremonial rite of spiritual rebirth and entry into the Christian faith. The practice of dressing infants in elaborate robes for christening began in England in the late seventeenth century and became increasingly common in America during the eighteenth century. In the early nineteenth century, infant dresses made of sheer cotton or linen embroidered with delicate floral patterns and lace inserts became the predominant style for christening dresses, a tradition that carried over into the twentieth century and even to the present day.[163]

The embroidery on this christening dress is in the manner of Ayrshire white work, a floral embroidery in satin stitch, stem stitch, and cutwork with needle lace. A large-scale industry developed in England, Scotland, and Ireland that employed thousands of female professional embroiderers working in their homes to produce huge quantities of this type of work to be sold in Britain, Europe, and the United States as a luxury textile. This style of embroidery, however, was also accessible to amateur embroiderers in America who used printed patterns found in ladies' journals and needlework books to create their own versions of this white-work style.[164]

Francis Henry Appleton (1847–1939) wore the embroidered dress and quilted booties to his christening at St. Paul's Church (Episocopal) in Boston on 1 November 1847. He was the first child born to Francis Henry Appleton (1823–54) and Georgiana Crowninshield Silsbee Appleton. Francis Henry Appleton attended the Bussey Agricultural Institute of Harvard College and operated a farm for many years in Peabody, Massachusetts, noted for breeding cattle and chickens. He joined the First Corps of Cadets in 1879 and eventually attained the rank of major general. General Appleton was a representative to the General Court and served in the Massachusetts Senate in 1902 and 1903. He died in Boston in 1939 at the age of 91.[165]

49

Needlework portrait of George Washington (1852)
by Sarah Sprague Dole Poor (1819–81)
Somerville, Massachusetts
Wool, cotton, and linen; 51 x 42 in.
Gift of Mrs. John J. Richards Jr., 1963
130567

Following his death in 1799, President George Washington took on the mythic stature in American popular culture that continues to the present day. In the early nineteenth century, memorial prints and embroideries commemorated his death, apotheosized him from a mortal man to the father of his country, and allegorized him as an emblem of the new American republic. Washington's popularity did not wane in the nineteenth century, and his portrait continued to be the subject of embroideries throughout the century.[166]

This portrait worked by Sarah Sprague Dole Poor in 1852 adapts the portrait of George Washington painted by the American artist John Trumbull (1756–1841) in 1792. It depicts General Washington on the eve of battle in 1778 surveying the British occupation of Trenton, New Jersey, that American troops had just evacuated. The decisive victory at Princeton the following day marked a turning point in the American Revolution. Shortly after the battle, English and American publishers and engravers replicated the original painting, and these prints formed the basis for embroidery patterns.[167] Individual pattern makers and embroiderers exercised considerable latitude in the selection and adaptation of the design, coloration, technique, and finishing. These options provide unique attributes to works derived from the same visual source. The reproduction of oil paintings by famous artists in embroidery had its roots in the English genre of "needlepainting" that flourished in the late eighteenth and early nineteenth centuries. In the nineteenth century, large pictures of heroic scenes or important figures worked in Berlin wool work continued this tradition.[168]

The maker, Sarah Sprague Dole Poor, was born in Danvers, Massachusetts, the daughter of Moses and Sarah Boardman Titcomb Dole. In 1840, she married John Robinson Poor (1818–81), and the couple had four children. Her third child, a daughter, was born in the same year that Sarah Poor completed the embroidered portrait. John Robinson Poor began in the grocery business, but in 1850, he established the partnership of Stickney and Poor that operated a firm purveying mustard, spices, and coffee in Charlestown and in Boston. The family resided in Somerville, Massachusetts, until around 1880 when they went west to California where Sarah Poor died in 1881 at the age of sixty-two.[169]

50

Ship portrait Marianne Nottebon *of New York* *(late nineteenth century)*
attributed to Thomas Willis (1850–1912)
New York
Oil paint, cotton, silk, and canvas; 26¼ x 38 in.
Gift of Gladys and Emily Safford, 1952
M6663

The Peabody Essex Museum owns a large and significant collection of ship portraits, a form of maritime art practiced in the eighteenth, nineteenth, and twentieth centuries. Often commissioned by the shipowners or captains, the vessels were depicted with a high degree of detail that included correct rigging, masts, the set of the sails, wind direction, and flags. The museum's collection contains numerous ship portraits done in watercolors and oil on canvas from many of the premier American, European, and Asian artists working in this genre, including Fitz Hugh Lane, James E. Buttersworth, Michele Felice Cornè, Antonio Jacobsen, the Roux family, Robert Salmon, and others.[170] This work is an unusual example of a ship portrait in a mixed medium that combines both painting and embroidery.

The artist, Thomas Willis, was born in Denmark and worked in Brooklyn, New York, as a marine artist. For a time, he apparently worked for a manufacturer of silk embroidery thread, and this may have influenced his choice of medium. He advertised as an "Inventor & sole maker of silk ware pictures." The works were noted for having textile hulls that were often in velvet. Sails were silk or satin. They had painted backgrounds and embroidered details such as waves, rigging, human figures, and other motifs. He often signed his work with a monogram that superimposed his initials.[171] Willis's superb handling of the medium makes his paintings indistinguishable from oil paintings at first glance. Upon close examination, the use of textiles and embroidery becomes apparent.

Built in New York in 1857, the ship *Marianne Nottebon* (sometimes spelled "Nottebohm") was 186 feet long and was registered at 1,116 tons. She operated for more than ten years as a transatlantic packet carrying passengers and cargo between New York and Liverpool. Later, she was engaged in the Pacific trade, sailing between Atlantic ports and San Francisco. In one notable run in 1869, the *Nottebon* sailed from New York to San Francisco in 118 days. Refitted as a coal barge after a forty-year career as a sailing vessel, the ship foundered off the Atlantic coast in 1902.[172]

51

Panel for a fire screen (1865–85)
by an unidentified artist
Salem, Massachusetts
Wool, glass, metal, and cotton; 31¹/₂ x 28 in.
Gift of Edward D. Lovejoy, 1946
122921

This large panel embroidered in wool and glass beads draws its inspiration from history paintings and genre scenes that were among the most popular art works produced in the nineteenth century. European and American artists created dramatic reenactments of historic events or literary subjects in imitation of Old Master paintings. These works, sometimes called "style troubadour," expressed romantic, chivalric, and sentimental ideals that appealed to middle- and upper-class patrons and consumers. Courtiers, cavaliers, and French musketeers of the seventeenth century were favored subjects due to the popularity of novels by authors such as Sir Walter Scott and Alexandre Dumas. Painters of genre scenes often utilized exacting finishing techniques to achieve highly detailed renderings of the subject. This was also true of embroiderers who worked similar subjects in textiles to be incorporated into the ornate interiors of the Victorian home.[173]

The fire-screen panel depicts a cavalier placing a ring on the finger of a lady in a dramatic and romantic gesture. The figures are entirely worked in colored glass beads with the exception of the flesh tones of their skin and the woman's purse. The subtle gradation of colors and the iridescent quality of the beads give the scene a shimmering, painterly effect. Metallic beads used for the ring, the handle of the woman's purse, and the tip of the cavalier's sword provide texture and dimension.

The panel was intended for use in a fire screen and would have been mounted in a frame attached to a base. The original purpose of fire screens was to shield people who sat close to open fireplaces. However, by the middle of the nineteenth century, with changes in heating technology, fire screens became largely ornamental furnishings and were frequently embellished with needlework. This fire-screen panel was originally used in the large Victorian mansion known as the Putnam-Balch House at 329 Essex Street in Salem, Massachusetts. The house was built for James S. Putnam during 1871 and 1872. It is an eclectic combination of the French academic and high Victorian Italianate styles.[174]

Chair-seat upholstery (1865–85)
by an unidentified artist
Probably Salem, Massachusetts
Wool, cotton, and glass; 21½ x 22 in.
Gift of Edward D. Lovejoy, 1946
122920

Domestic economy guides and decorating advice books of the nineteenth century advocated that upholstery be used to add comfort to home interiors and to demonstrate the family's awareness of the prevailing cultural and aesthetic tastes. Women from widely different economic backgrounds undertook upholstery projects as a means to improve their homes in an affordable and highly personal manner. Berlin wool work and canvas work were popular media for upholstery because of the availability of patterns and materials and the durability of the finished product.[175] Canvas-work upholstery based on prints or tapestry designs had been used in England and Europe since the sixteenth century, and this historical precedent appealed to the spirit of revivalism that dominated the decorative arts in the nineteenth century. The shells and C-scroll motifs in white interspersed among the flowers may reflect the rococo-revival style.[176]

This unused example of upholstery was probably intended for a chair seat or as a decorative cushion. The colors reflect the preference for vivid hues following the introduction of aniline or chemical dyes in textile production in the 1850s. The green background has an area that is in a slightly different shade of color that may indicate a variation in dye lots. Glass beading draws attention to the delicate vines and would have added a reflective quality when viewed by gaslight or candlelight. Katherine Grier has noted that beaded upholstery was used for furniture meant to be accent pieces within the decorative scheme of the room.[177]

It is not known who completed the embroidery of the chair seat. The donor of the upholstery also gave the museum the fire-screen panel (catalogue entry 51) at the same time, and it is possible that it was made for use in the house at 329 Essex Street in Salem, Massachusetts.

53

Mantel valance (1875–95)
by an unidentified artist
New England
Wool and silk; 11 x 52 in.
Gift of Miss E. Evans, 1928
119651

The hearth has occupied a central place in the American home since colonial times. In the nineteenth century, changes in heating technology reduced the functional need for fireplaces and gave new emphasis to the aesthetics of the hearth and mantel. Home furnishing guides promoted tasteful decorating and guided American women in how to create healthful and pleasing interiors on a budget. Soft furnishings such as curtains, cushions, table covers, and textile room accessories were advocated as means to enhance comfort and personalize the decorating scheme.[178]

Mantel valances were narrow textile panels that attached to the mantel shelf as decorative elements. The shape of the panel made it a popular subject for embroidery. This mantel valance features floral motifs interspersed with Gothic arches and trefoils in a tracery pattern. The Gothic Revival style adapted design elements of late medieval architecture and decorative arts, and it became one of several design precedents that were incorporated into the Arts and Crafts movement. Constance Cary Harrison in *Women's Handiwork in Modern Homes* (1881) advocated adapting fifteenth-century illuminated manuscripts that combine flowers and fruit with lozenge-shaped motifs and arabesques.[179]
"Art needlework," first popularized by the display of needlework from the Royal School of Art Needlework at the Centennial Exhibition in Philadelphia in 1876, prompted a revival of crewel embroidery.[180]
The floral motifs of tulips, daffodils, and hyacinths emulate Elizabethan embroideries of the sixteenth century. This mantel valance is unfinished and unused, two factors that contributed to the retention of its bright colors and its remarkably good condition.

54

Valance (1875–85)
by an unidentified artist
New England
Wool, canvas, wood, silk, and glass beads; 14 x 21¼ in.
Gift of Mrs. Shepard D. Gilbert, 1947
126547

In the *American Woman's Home* (1869), Catherine E. Beecher and Harriet Beecher Stowe noted that the decoration of houses "contributes much to the education of the entire household in refinement, intellectual development, and moral sensibility." Interior decoration became a means to elevate the American family's intellectual, social, aesthetic, and moral advancement. Fueled by this view, nineteenth-century American women used embroidery, upholstery, and other textiles in the Arts and Crafts style to create interiors that embodied these ideals.[181]

Parlors and other rooms in nineteenth-century houses were swathed in functional and ornamental textiles. Berlin wool work or needlepoint was particularly popular for upholstery because it was sturdy, easily worked, and "capable of good results." Advances in printing technology made Berlin-work patterns affordable and readily available. Although much maligned when it fell from favor at the end of the nineteenth century, Berlin wool work in the hands of inspired designers and embroiderers could be used to create works of considerable beauty.[182]

This valance or lambrequin features floral sprays and a leafy vine worked in richly colored wools. Iridescent bluish-gray glass beads form the background around the flowers and create a shimmering surface that reflects light. Fancy silk tassels and two-colored silk cording finish the edges of the valance and add to the texture of the embroidery. Illustrations in the book *Beautiful Homes; or, Hints in Home Furnishings* (1878) show a similar valance suspended from a windowsill as part of an elaborate set of curtains. Similar valances were also attached to shelves.[183]

55

Dress (ca. 1880)
by an unidentified artist
United States
Wool, silk, linen, and cotton; 55 in. (length)
Gift of David O. Ives, 1976
133939

This dress features embroidery of pink and red roses and blue forget-me-nots in a style of needlework popular in the late nineteenth century known as "art needlework." Art needlework was a manifestation of the Arts and Crafts movement that gained popularity in England in the third quarter of the nineteenth century. It revived crewel embroidery rather than counted-thread techniques and employed skillful shading of color and varying textures to create a more painterly effect. Americans received exposure to this new style at the Centennial Exhibition held in Philadelphia in 1876 through displays of needlework sponsored by the Royal School of Art and Needlework under the patronage of Queen Victoria.[184]

The glossy silk embroidery contrasts with the soft, dull finish of the dark green wool ground. The floral motifs of roses and forget-me-nots may allude to the nineteenth-century language of flowers described by one author as "a coded language of love." Floral lexicons that associated various meanings or sentiments with individual flowers and plants were popular gifts to women throughout the nineteenth century. Recent scholarship indicates that it was a widely understood cultural and artistic practice in America. The rose was usually associated with love or beauty, and the forget-me-not meant what its name implies.[185]

The embroidery may have been the work of a professional embroiderer working abroad. Embroidered dress components made in European fashion centers were exported to the United States where they could be purchased by consumers and taken to dressmakers for custom fitting and construction. Imported goods often served as inspiration for American-made products. Family tradition suggests that the dress belonged originally to Mrs. Albert P. (Sarah Braden) Goodhue (1844–1918) of Salem, Massachusetts, the grandmother of the donor.

56

Table cover (1870–80)
Mrs. Josiah (Eliza Tufts) Brodhead (1831–1900)
Probably Boston, Massachusetts
Silk and wool; 62 x 62 in.
Gift of Mrs. Paul T. Haskell, Mrs. John Pickering, and Mrs. James J. Storrow, 1960
129730

The center table was the focal point of the parlor in nineteenth-century America, and it embodied symbolic meanings about families and parlor culture as well as serving a functional purpose. Historian Katherine Grier identified center tables as "shrines within the ritual space of the parlor." It was frequently the location for a lamp that provided the most brightly illuminated area in the room and consequently was the gathering place of the family after dark. Grier also notes that an appropriate table cover "could qualify any table for center table use, even one that was roughly made."[186] Consequently, rich and colorful textiles and hand-wrought embellishments were extensively used on table covers to signify the importance of their role within the home. In the second half of the nineteenth century, covers that featured border patterns with plain centers found favor because they allowed the table to accommodate treasured family objects such as photograph albums, books, sewing boxes, and decorative objects.[187]

A beautifully rendered border of embroidered blackberry vines surrounds a central panel of blue silk satin.[188] Decorative stitching in a variation of the featherstitch finishes the seam. A three-colored fringe of silk tassels binds the outside edge of the table cover. The design is in the style of "art needlework" that gained favor with American embroiderers in the 1870s. *The Dictionary of Needlework* (1882) defines art needlework as "a name recently introduced as a general term for all descriptions of needlework that spring from the application of a knowledge of design and colouring." It also notes that "much individual scope in execution and colouring is required from the embroiderer."[189]

The maker of the table cover was Eliza Tufts Brodhead, wife of Colonel Josiah Adams Brodhead of Boston. Colonel Brodhead served in the army during the Civil War, and after the war continued in military service as a paymaster in California and other posts in the West. He died in Boston shortly after returning from Tucson, Arizona, in 1884.[190] The Brodheads had three daughters. For several years before her death in 1900, Mrs. Brodhead lived in Salem with her daughter Rebecca and her husband, Henry P. Benson, who became mayor of Salem.[191]

57

Banner screen *(1875–1900)*
by Mrs. Nathaniel A. (Harriet M.) Horton (1832–1908)
Salem, Massachusetts
Silk, wool, and brass; 26 x 12 in.
Gift of William A. Horton, 1921
113969

Banner screens, along with fire screens, tea screens, and lamp screens, were used in nineteenth-century parlors or reception rooms to provide shade from light and heat emanating from fireplaces, windows, and lamps. Constance Cary Harrison in *Women's Handiwork in Modern Homes* (1881) advocated the use of banner screens "where it is desirable to relieve the eye from constant contemplation of bright hues and warm fabrics." They also served as decorative ornaments that were favorite subjects for embroidery.[192]

The scene on this banner screen is a woman in classical dress worked in outline stitch or stem stitch on a silk background. Outline stitch emphasized the linearity and silhouette of the design without the use of shading or variations in color. Constance Cary Harrison asserted that "Outline work is independent of color; knows not the aid of light and shadow; gives only suggestions of beauty in pure and simple curves." She also noted that designs by artists such as Englishman John Flaxman (1755–1826) "of the human figure, in illustration of Roman and Greek mythology, are to be had from dealers in artists' supplies" and "afford a valuable addition to the art-worker's portfolio."[193] The "Pompeian" style that intermingled elements of ancient Greek and Roman art was one of the eclectic revivals favored in architecture, decorative arts, and interior furnishings at the end of the nineteenth century.[194]

The embroidered panel is inserted between two borders of rich, dark red plush velvet. The seams have been embellished with fancy stitching variations of the featherstitch that was frequently used on crazy quilts. The upper edge of the panel is attached to a brass rod, and the lower edge is finished with long wool fringe.[195]

Mrs. Harriet M. Horton, the maker of the banner screen, was the wife of Nathaniel A. Horton (1830–1901), editor of the *Salem Gazette* and a Massachusetts state senator. The couple married in 1854 and had two children, a daughter and a son. Her obituary in the *Salem Evening News* described her as a "genial, kind hearted woman, with a pleasant greeting for all." It also noted that she was active in many charitable organizations, including the Woman's Alliance of the Second Church, Salem.[196]

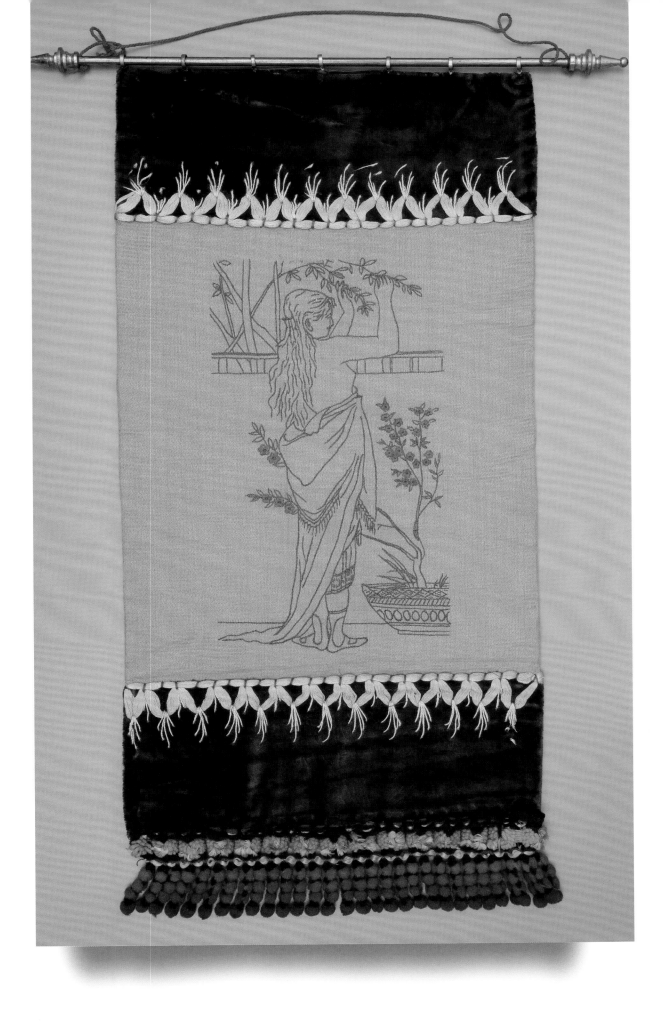

58

Table cover (1885–95)
by an unidentified artist
New England
Silk, metallic thread, and cotton; 60$\frac{1}{2}$ x 61$\frac{1}{2}$ in.
Gift of Ellen Moulton, 1944
125860

The design of this large table cover shows the influence of the Arts and Crafts movement that flourished in England and America between the 1870s and 1920. Brought to prominence by English designers such as William Morris (1834–96), the Arts and Crafts style drew on a number of diverse artistic influences including ecclesiastical embroidery of the Middle Ages; "exotic" cultures including the Near East, India, Persia, and Japan; historic references to embroideries of the Renaissance period through the eighteenth century; and designs adapted from nature. Design elements based on plant life were among the most popular patterns for embroidery and other textiles.[197]

A wide border of embroidered flowers worked in silk and gold metallic thread on satin extends around the perimeter of the table cover. Large tulips are interspersed with jonquils on an undulating vine. The corners feature a triangular motif of three star-shaped flowers. The central panel is made of ribbed moiré or watered silk. A large tricolored silk ball fringe hangs from the mauve plush or velvet band along the outer edge of the table cover. One instruction book of 1884 notes that the edges of table covers could be "trimmed with plush balls, either all one color, or different colors alternating, care being taken not to have the balls too near together." The quality of the design and materials suggest that this may be the work of a professional embroiderer or a highly trained amateur. Art needlework schools and decorative arts societies in both England and America produced exceptional embroideries made on commission for individual patrons or available for purchase by the public.[198]

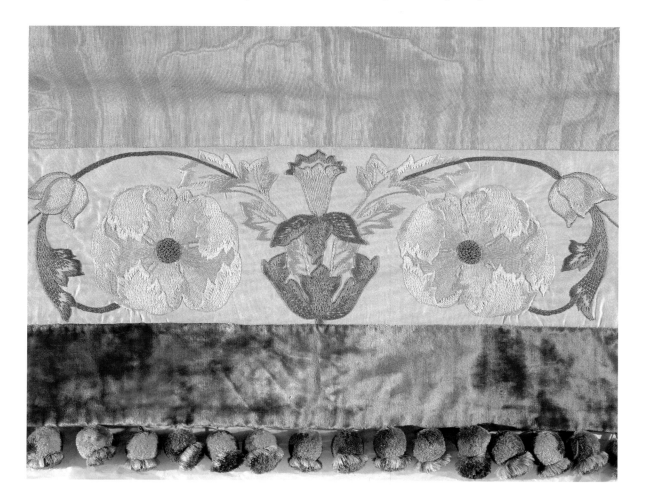

59

Dress *(ca. 1895)*
by Eliza Philbrick (1836–1927)
Salem, Massachusetts
Wool, linen, brass, and cotton; 56 in. (length)
Gift of Eliza Philbrick, 1919
109674

The dress made by Eliza Philbrick of Salem, Massachusetts, embodies layers of family history and meaning. It exemplifies the ideals of the Colonial Revival, an artistic and cultural movement in which America's colonial past was reformulated to communicate ideas about patriotism and national identity at the turn of the century. When she donated the dress to the Essex Institute in 1919, Miss Philbrick inscribed its history on a paper tag attached to the garment. "This gown was made from a web of cloth woven in a hand-loom at my Grandfather's, Judge Joseph Philbrick's, at Weare, N.H.—before 1810. It is pressed woolen cloth camwood color. The band of embroidery on skirt is a copy of a piece that was hand wrought, before the Revolutionary War, and was embroidered by Eliza Philbrick. The cloth remained uncut in the piece for over ninety years when it was made up in one of the Revolutionary styles to wear to a Colonial Costume party of the 'Daughters of the Revolution' in Boston."[199]

Eliza Philbrick was photographed wearing the dress in 1898 and in 1911, and her handwritten captions on the photographs reveal that she altered the dress at least once.[200] When she made the dress around 1895, the embroidered panel on the skirt was a historic textile, a long narrow strip that may once have been part of a bed valence or petticoat border of the eighteenth century. This embroidered panel is now in the collections of the Beverly (Massachusetts) Historical Society.[201] Sometime before 1911, Miss Philbrick removed the embroidered band and replaced it with an exact reproduction that she had stitched herself. She also added a matching embroidered collar and cuffs.

Eliza Philbrick's obituary notes that she was always interested "especially in antiquary."[202] In 1897, she published an article on "Spinning in the Olden Time" that reveals her significant knowledge about textiles in early America and offers insight into the meaning of her dress. She records that at the time of the American Revolution, "garments made of fabrics spun by the young lady weavers' own hands were emulously worn as proofs of patriotism."[203] By constructing the dress from fabric handmade by her ancestors and creating embroidery in an exact replica of a historical design, Miss Philbrick communicates pride in her family's heritage and makes a statement about American identity. The aesthetics of the Colonial Revival often combine design elements and motifs from the eighteenth century with the neoclassicism of the American Federal period. Although Eliza Philbrick sought to recreate a "colonial" dress, the raised waistline and pleated bodice are more closely associated with women's garments of the early nineteenth century. The woolen fabric, however, is the embodiment of "homespun." As such, it symbolized the patriotism, industry, and frugality of the early settlers in the minds of late-nineteenth-century Americans who were grappling with the effects of industrialization, urbanization, and immigration.[204]

Eliza Philbrick was the fifth of ten children born to farmer Joseph Philbrick (1796–1863) and his wife, Clara (1803–86), of Seabrook, New Hampshire. The farmhouse owned by her grandparents, Joseph Philbrick (1772–1830) and Hannah (Gove) Philbrick (1774–1838), still stands in Weare, New Hampshire. The Philbrick family raised sheep, processed wool, and wove cloth at the farm in the late eighteenth and early nineteenth century.[205] In adulthood, Eliza lived in Salem, Massachusetts, with her sister Climena (b. 1840) and was a member of the Essex Institute and the Daughters of the American Revolution.

60

Set of doilies (1899–1905)
by Mable Clare Hillyer Pollock (1884–1963)
Ohio or Massachusetts
Silk on linen; 15 and 9 in. in diameter
Gift of the estate of Mable Clare Hillyer Pollock, 1963
130484.1–4

Around 1900, a new phase of art needlework called "silk work" became popular for use with table linens, doilies, and household textiles used in middle-class American homes. Inspired by British art needlework, silk work was also influenced by Asian art and textile traditions, especially Japanese embroidery and Chinese embroidered shawls that featured realistic floral designs.[206] It also coincided with the wave of interest of American women in gardening, horticulture, and botany, and some embroidery books included explanations of plant anatomy as well as stitching instructions.[207] It also encompassed eclectic design references to other artistic movements favored at the turn of the century, including the rococo revival and art nouveau. Silk work utilized "Asiatic Dye" or wash silk thread that was noted for its production in hundreds of color shades, colorfastness during washing, and a glossy sheen that contrasted well with white and colored linens.

American textile manufacturers hired professional women artists, designers, and writers to produce embroidery books, patterns, and instructions for working art embroidery, sometimes noting the artists' names with their original designs.[208] Although women could purchase stamped linens at drygoods and department stores, art embroidery encouraged the personalization of these textiles by the selection of materials, the color shading, and the mastery of embroidery techniques that enhanced the intent of the design. When integrated with other furnishings in a well-appointed American home or used in domestic social ceremonies, these textiles exemplified the artistic and cultural awareness of the maker and her family.[209]

Mable Clare Hillyer Pollock was born in Ashtabula, Ohio. She received training as an artist at the Pratt Institute in New York. She served as a teacher of art in Salem public and vocational schools until her marriage in 1925. She later taught watercolor and oil painting and decorative painting on trays. She was a member of the Copley Art Society of Boston.[210]

61

Evening cape (1900–1910)
by Liberty and Company
London
Wool and silk; 65 in. (length)
Gift of Mr. and Mrs. S. Morton Vose, 1998
137950

The pink wool-and-silk evening cape reflects the influence of the Arts and Crafts movement on clothing design in the early twentieth century. Motivated by a desire to overturn the effects of industrialization and the rigidity of the academic art establishment, artists and designers in the late nineteenth and early twentieth centuries adopted new aesthetic theories and styles and revived centuries-old craftsmanship techniques. Originating in England and quickly embraced in America, the Arts and Crafts style produced objects that drew on historical precedents adapted for modern life.[211]

The cape is in the form of a cope, a medieval liturgical garment made of rich fabrics and ornamented with embroidery. Semicircular in shape, it opens along the center front that is embellished with a broad border of embroidered and appliquéd floral motifs imitating an orphrey or decorative band. The simple form of the garment and the semiabstract style of the embroidery also suggest the beginnings of modernism, a style that became increasingly popular in the twentieth century.[212]

Mrs. Charles Storrow (1858–1943) of Brookline, Massachusetts, purchased the cape at Liberty and Company, the fashionable London retail shop. Founded in 1875 by Arthur Lasenby Liberty, the firm purchased furnishing textiles, needlework, and clothing from the leading designers of the day and became a noted proponent of the Arts and Crafts style.[213]

62

Original artwork for needlework patterns (1910–15)
by Jenny Brooks (1866–1937)
Salem, Massachusetts
Watercolor, ink, pencil, and paper; 13 x 10 in.
Gift of Mrs. Peter Shyte, 1963
130217

Following the success of organizations such as the Deerfield Blue and White Society that developed a cottage industry in the 1890s producing textiles that combined colonial designs with the aesthetics of the Arts and Crafts movement, new professional opportunities in the burgeoning needlework industry became available to women. With the widespread demand for needlework patterns distributed in magazines or those published by textile companies for distribution through drygoods shops and department stores, female needlework artists and designers increased in number.[214] In Salem, Massachusetts, the Jenny Brooks Company produced embroidery patterns in the Colonial Revival style from the 1890s through the first World War. The museum's collection includes numerous examples of the firm's commercially printed patterns and also a smaller group of pieces of original art for embroidery patterns.

Jenny Brooks (1866–1937) went into partnership in 1893 with Edith Morse as designers of embroidery in the firm called Morse and Brooks. They kept an office in the Studio Building at 2 Chestnut Street, locally renowned for providing studio and classroom space to a number of artists, including Frank W. Benson and Philip Little.[215] They remained in partnership until 1898 when Jenny Brooks continued on with the firm under her own name. She maintained a shop at 1 Cambridge Street in Salem and seems to have ended her business activities around 1918. The firm produced cross-stitch patterns that could be adapted for use on table linens, other household textiles, and clothing. The patterns feature slightly abstracted designs of floral baskets, swags, antique objects, galleons and other sailing ships, and small devices such as insects, colonial people, and floral motifs. The aesthetics of this style draw from the colonial idiom and also from the spirit of abstraction and modernism that emerged in the early decades of the twentieth century.[216]

Jenny Brooks was the daughter of Henry Mason Brooks (1822–98) and Mary Matilda (Nichols) Brooks (d. 1895). Her father was a historian, antiquarian, musician, and museum curator of the Essex Institute. Her sisters included artist and teacher Mary Mason Brooks (1860–1915) and science writer Margarette Ward Brooks.[217]

63

Sampler *(1915)*
by Mary Saltonstall Parker (1850–1920)
Salem, Massachusetts
Cotton and linen; 21 ¼ x 14 ¼ in.
Gift of Mrs. Francis T. Parker, 1979
134863

In 1923, author Mary Harrod Northend described the samplers designed and made by her Salem neighbor Mary Saltonstall Parker in the periodical *International Studio.* She maintained that "There is something distinctive about the new samplers, perhaps the artful combination of the old and the new. . . . She has preserved in them the charming naiveté of spirit of the needlework of her ancestors but has developed a technique that is quite superior to that of most of the pieces of the generations long gone." Northend also noted that "she has made in her samplers reference to or records of contemporary events or incidents which doubtless will be interesting to future students of domestic art."[218] This sampler—begun in 1914 and completed in 1915—expresses Parker's thoughts about World War I prior to the involvement of the United States in the war effort.

Born into a prominent Salem family, Mary Saltonstall Tuckerman Parker attended the private schools kept by Miss Caroline H. King and Miss Jane Phillips. As a young woman, she received additional training in art needlework at classes held in private homes in Salem. In 1887, she married William Phineas Parker (1855–1923), a businessman and cousin of Salem's famous Parker Brothers, the game manufacturers, and the couple had two children. In the 1890s, Parker authored and published several brief books on Colonial Revival themes. In the first decade of the twentieth century, Parker resumed embroidery again, focusing on the production of Colonial Revival samplers. Beginning around 1907, Parker designed and produced at least one sampler each year until her death in 1920. Initially, she adapted commercially printed patterns, arranging individual motifs around verses from favorite authors or rhyming verse that she composed herself. After 1910, she began to draw original patterns, and her work received the attention of national magazines as well as local and regional newspapers.[219]

In October of 1915, the magazine *House Beautiful* featured an article by Katherine Gauss, "Contemporary History in Cross-Stitch," that featured photographs of Mary Parker's samplers. A caption for this sampler explains Parker's intent. The sampler is divided into four registers or horizontal bands. The upper section features verses and motifs that represent "the peace and prosperity of the United States." The second tier depicts emblems of the European nations engaged in conflict: Germany (imperial eagle), Great Britain (lion), France (fleur-de-lis), and Russia (bear). The third register portrays machines of war, such as battleships and airplanes, and the ruins of Rheims cathedral. These motifs were interspersed with biblical verses. Along the right side, a band of soldiers march to the popular wartime tune "It's a Long Way to Tipperary." The bottom section shows women at home and sentinels manning cannons waiting for the hostilities to end.[220] Parker's use of emblems and symbolic motifs interspersed with literary quotes makes her samplers distinctive examples of Colonial Revival needlework that both emulates and departs from the embroidery traditions of early America.

64

Sampler (1918)
by Mary Saltonstall Parker (1856–1920)
Salem, Massachusetts
Cotton and linen; 20^1/$_4$ x 11^5/$_8$ in.
Gift of Mrs. Francis Tuckerman Parker, 1980
135061

In the early twentieth century, the Colonial Revival renewed interest in American samplers, both as relics of the past and as a vibrant form of contemporary cultural expression. Freed from its role as an educational exercise for schoolgirls, the making of samplers became a vehicle for adult women to express their opinions on social, political, and domestic themes.[221] Among the most inventive artists working in this genre was Mary Saltonstall Parker (1856–1920) of Salem, Massachusetts. National publications such as *House Beautiful* and *International Studio* featured Parker's samplers as magazine covers and as illustrations for articles. Her works combine qualities distinctive of Colonial Revival samplers including "old-fashioned subjects with modern-day tendencies."[222] This sampler, one of two Parker designed and made to commemorate World War I, exemplifies these traits.

Parker probably commenced this sampler following the enlistment of her two sons in the spring of 1918. The upper register of the sampler records the names and enlistment dates of her father in 1842 and that of her older son, Francis Tuckerman Parker, who served in the United States Navy, and of the younger, William Bradstreet Parker, who joined the army. The middle of the sampler is filled with images of war: tents, marching soldiers, bands of stars and stripes, service stars, warships, and artillery shells. Parker adapted some of these devices from commercial patterns, and others were her original designs. For the large sailing ship at the bottom of the sampler, Parker used imagery from the Bayeux tapestry that recorded the Norman conquest of England by William the Conqueror in 1066. By this allusion to an ancient embroidered historical narrative, Parker equates her own embroidered expressions with those of Queen Mathilda, the supposed maker of the Bayeux tapestry.[223] The inscription records the role of women in wartime who "Keep the Home Fires burning Till the Boys Come Home." It also records her relief at completing the sampler shortly after the armistice in November of 1918 "in the Dawn of Peace."

65

Sampler *(1920)*
by Mary Saltonstall Parker (1856–1920)
Salem, Massachusetts
Cotton and linen; 27 x 20 in.
Gift of Mrs. Francis Tuckerman Parker, 1980
135057

The final sampler that Mary Saltonstall Parker completed in 1920 is a complex expression about aging, illness, and the approach of death. To some extent, the pastel color scheme and the use of small emblems disguise the expressiveness of the object. However, careful consideration of the symbolism encoded in the motifs and the selection of the verses reveal the ability of the artist to use a sampler to communicate deep and highly personal messages.

The upper register of the sampler features a poem by Matthew Prior:

Great Mother, let me once be able

To Have a Garden, House, and Stable,

That I may read, and ride, and plant,

Superior to desire, or want;

And as health fails, and years increase,

Sit down, and think and die in peace.

The poem trails around a pastoral landscape that recalls the embroidered "fishing lady pictures" worked in Boston in the eighteenth century. The influence of the Colonial Revival style can be seen in this reference to early American needlework and in the emblems such as the "Carver" chair, associated with Governor John Carver, a passenger on the Mayflower and first governor of the Plymouth Colony. The hourglass is an allusion to timekeeping in a preindustrial age and also a symbol of the passage of time in an individual life.[224]

The second verses are taken from John Bunyan's *The Pilgrim's Progress,* an allegory on human life and Christian salvation published in two parts in 1678 and 1684. *The Pilgrim's Progress* grew in popularity following Bunyan's death in 1688 and was one of the most widely read Protestant texts in nineteenth-century America.[225] The verses and images selected by Mrs. Parker reflect the idea of pilgrimage, neighborly care and companionship, and peace at journey's end.

The bottom of the sampler contains diverse imagery and symbols that express several ideas. Two patron saints occupy the lower left corner, suggesting the comfort of religion. Saint Elizabeth of Hungary, who carries a basket of roses, was noted for self-sacrifice and for attending to the needs of the poor and sick. The bishop is probably St. Ambrose, the fourth-century cleric noted as a theologian, the originator of the Ambrosian chant, and a religious poet.[226] Patriotic emblems, the shield with stars and stripes, the motto "Armistice," and the eagle of victory celebrate the recent end of World War I. At the very bottom of the sampler, on either side of her name, Parker stitched a candlestick with a candle that has just been snuffed out. This motif was adapted from a pattern published by Anne Orr that was designed for use on a tray or table cover "to place by the invalid's bed at night."[227] Mary Parker reinterpreted this element and seems to use it to communicate her awareness of the approach of the end of her life. Mary Saltonstall Parker's original sketches for her samplers as well as her library of published needlework patterns are in the collections of the Phillips Library of the Peabody Essex Museum.[228]

Great Mother, let me once be able
To have a Garden, House, and Stable,
That I may read, and ride, and plant,
Superior to desire, or want;

And as health falls, and years increase,

Sit down, and think, and die in peace.

Matthew Prior.

So she (Mercy) said within herself, If my neighbor will needs be gone, I will go a little way with her and help her.

Saint Elizabeth.

Bunyan

A Shepherd of Souls.

1920

A large upper Chamber whose toward the Sun-Rising: the name of the Chamber was PEACE.

The Mill will never grind with the water that has passed.

Bunyan

Mary Saltonstall Parker

Armistice

VICTORY

131

The Fishing Lady (1939)
by Nannie Jenks Borden Phillips (1877–1963)
Topsfield, Massachusetts
Wool, canvas, wood, gilding, and glass; 34^1/$_2$ x 55 in.
Gift of the estate of Nannie Jenks Borden Phillips, 1963
130442

Exact replication of historic needlework has been a widely practiced genre of embroidery in the last half of the twentieth century. Although initially a manifestation of the Colonial Revival, its popularity has persisted long after other techniques associated with the Arts and Crafts movement have waned. Unlike the Colonial Revival works of the early twentieth century, the purpose of reproduction needlework is to recreate the experience and values of the past as well as the construction of a mimetic object. As antique needlework has become increasingly scarce and its monetary value has increased, this trend has enabled many embroiderers to own textiles that appear old and incorporate them into historically inspired interior decorating schemes.[229]

The large needlepoint picture entitled *The Fishing Lady* completed by Nannie Jenks Borden Phillips in 1939 is an impressive reproduction, both in terms of its size and accuracy. It is "an exact copy" of the chimneypiece made by Eunice Bourne (b. 1732) of Barnstable, Massachusetts, in 1748 now in the collections of the Museum of Fine Arts, Boston. Helen Bowen in her article "The Fishing Lady and Boston Common" published in the magazine *Antiques* in August of 1923 noted a group of embroideries that featured the same motif of a woman fishing and other related design elements. Mrs. Phillips may have known of the piece from the magazine article but must certainly have seen the original at the museum in Boston at some point. It appears that she attempted to recreate the more vibrant colors of the Bourne chimneypiece as it was originally made rather than copying the faded hues. She also had the original frame reproduced to complete the presentation of her needlework.[230]

Having completed this work in 1939, Nannie Jenks Borden Phillips embarked on a second large-scale landscape scene, *Our Safari*, based on a trip to Africa in 1930. A comparison of the two works gives insight into the broad artistic and cultural traditions that inspired both embroideries. Although much documentation survives about the design and construction of the later work, little information has been discovered to date about the earlier landscape.

Nannie Jenks Borden Phillips was the wife of historian and author James Duncan Phillips (1876–1954) who wrote numerous articles and books, including *Salem in the Eighteenth Century* (1937). The oil portrait of Mrs. Phillips that appears below is by Edith Cleaves Barry (1884–1969). The couple lived in a historic farmhouse in Topsfield, Massachusetts.

67

Our Safari (1940–44)
by Nannie Jenks Borden Phillips (1877–1963)
Topsfield, Massachusetts
Wool, canvas, and painted wood; 34$^1/_2$ x 55 in.
Gift of the estate of Nannie Jenks Borden Phillips, 1963
130443

Embroidery in the twentieth century became increasingly used as a vehicle for self-expression.[231] *Our Safari* records sights and impressions of Africa experienced by the artist Nannie Jenks Borden Phillips during an automobile journey made with her husband and two traveling companions in 1930 and 1931. In 1947, Mrs. Phillips exhibited the large needlepoint tapestry in the fiftieth anniversary exhibition of the Society of Arts and Crafts in Boston. In the entry paperwork for the exhibition, she recorded that she developed the original designs from photographs taken in Kenya, Uganda, and Sudan by her traveling companion Katherine Wellman of Topsfield, Massachusetts. Original photographs by Wellman and a few pencil sketches or patterns done by Mrs. Phillips are in the collections of the Stephen Phillips Trust House, Salem, Massachusetts. The photographs include the picture of the artist and her husband in front of a thatched hut that Mrs. Phillips adapted into a self-portrait at the right center of the needlework. The three mountains in the background are the Mountain of the Moon (left), Mount Kilimanjaro (center), and Mount Kenya (right). The Nile River is in the lower left corner and Lake Bunyoni in Uganda is at the center right. When it was exhibited in 1947, Mrs. Phillips set the valuation of the work at five thousand dollars.[232]

Born in Fall River, Massachusetts, Nannie Jenks Borden Phillips married historian and author James Duncan Phillips in 1907 in Headcorn, Kent, England. He held several offices at the publishing firm of Houghton Mifflin Company in Boston from 1898 to 1942. The couple traveled extensively in North and Central America, Europe, Asia, and Australia.[233] Mrs. Phillips pursued a variety of artistic endeavors. She is listed in the exhibition records of the Society of Arts and Crafts of Boston as a toy maker in 1916 and 1917.[234] In 1932, she exhibited ceramics at the Pottery Workshop of Boston at 79 Chestnut Street that operated under the direction of George C. Greener. Among her surviving ceramics are a bowl that depicts a map of Africa and a series of plates that feature African animals. Some of the plates display the mark of the Paul Revere Pottery of Boston that operated between 1908 and 1942.[235] She also participated in social and voluntary organizations.

A detail of *Our Safari* showing the artist and her husband.
The full image appears on the following pages.

SUDAN UGANDA

68

Blanket: Wrapped in My Parents' Love (2000)
by Linda Behar
Massachusetts
Wool and cotton; 63 x 93 in. (flat); 63 x 82 x 6 in. (draped for display)
Museum purchase, 2000
138136

In the second half of the twentieth century, textile artists have struggled to emerge from the debate about whether embroidery and other textile techniques are an art or a craft. As definitions about art evolve and artists explore new uses for embroidery, the medium has moved far beyond the perceived limitations of earlier times. Fiber arts author and editor Nancy Orban and her colleagues have written that "contemporary artists now ask which mediums are appropriate for what they want to say, rather than letting particular mediums define their message."[236]

In the work entitled *Blanket: Wrapped in My Parents' Love,* artist Linda Behar embarked on a journey of self-discovery by revisiting another time in her life through adapting and reworking family photographs in embroidery to gain new insight into family relationships and dynamics. The work depicts a family portrait of the artist in her early childhood years with her parents. Ms. Behar made this commentary on her deeply personal work: "For the first time I learned that there was a period of my life—early, before siblings arrived—when I was the apple of my parents' eyes. I wished to be able to wrap myself in this newfound love. This blanket was the fruit of that desire."[237]

Many contemporary artists employ computers and work in multiple mediums to achieve specific aesthetic effects and conceptual intent.[238] Linda Behar often uses photography, painting, embroidery, and quilting to create her works. For this piece, she used the computer to retouch photographs and manipulate design elements and then developed a pattern that could be stitched in a counted cross-stitch technique. She evaluated her outcome in this fashion: "Interestingly, what appeared to be highly stylized images in the hard-edged computer print-out regained their organic nature when stitched in soft wool."[239]

Behar began her career as a quilt artist in the early 1980s and has worked primarily in embroidery for the last decade. Many of her previous works have been miniature in scale—the size of postcards—with thousands of tiny stitches that create impressionistic scenes of landscapes and still lifes.[240] This work was a departure from her earlier style in terms of scale, technique, and form. She has used a functional object, a blanket, as the ground fabric for the embroidery and worked the design in large counted cross-stitch, intentionally using traditional forms and techniques in new ways for her aesthetic purpose. The blanket is displayed draped, following the artist's instructions to emphasize the visual messages she wished to convey.

Needlecraft and Wollstonecraft:

A Case Study of Women's Rights and Education in Federal-Period Salem, Massachusetts

by Elysa Engelman

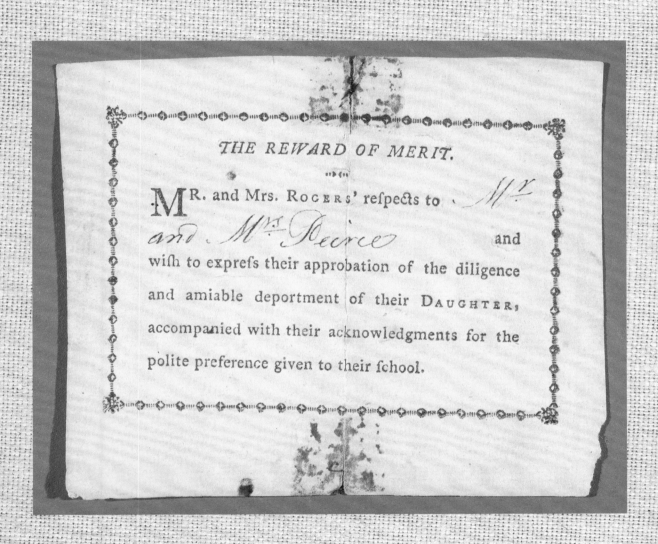

> ### THE REWARD OF MERIT.
>
> **M**R. and MRS. ROGERS' respects to *Mr.* and *Mrs. Peirce* and wish to express their approbation of the diligence and amiable deportment of their DAUGHTER, accompanied with their acknowledgments for the polite preference given to their school.

Throughout the summer of 1797, fifteen-year-old Sarah Peirce labored over her masterpiece in thread, a coat of arms worked on a field of satin. By the time she finished in September, this elaborate piece broadcast a number of messages about Sally and her family. Most obviously, it spoke of female accomplishment at a time when very few girls in Salem, or even Boston, progressed beyond practical needlework to the purely ornamental. Beginning with instruction in plain sewing, a girl learned to embroider initials on linen and to hem, mend, and darn her family's clothing and bedding. If she had the patience, time, and skill, at about the age of ten or twelve, she would complete a colorful sampler displaying her full repertoire of stitches. This sampler was both her final examination and diploma, suitable for framing and hanging on a wall. Only the wealthiest girls, those like Sally Peirce—whose father was a successful merchant—continued on for private instruction in needlecraft and tackled complex projects such as a coat of arms.

Sally's masterpiece testifies to her teacher's ability as much as to her own skill. Although she probably attended several Salem schools during her early teens, the records reveal only one of Sally's teachers by name: Mrs. Abigail Rogers. Mrs. Rogers was herself the well-educated daughter of a prominent local family, but had fallen on hard times after her marriage. For almost thirty years, she made a living by passing on her genteel skills to the next generation. Sally was her pupil in 1792 and 1793 and became a close friend thereafter. Quite possibly, Mrs. Rogers's hand guided the girl through her final project four years later.[241]

No one knows who decided that the family coat of arms and not another equally challenging pattern should become Sally's masterpiece—the teacher, the pupil, or her parents—but it was an appropriate choice for a girl from a wealthy family. Captain Jerathmiel Peirce could afford the expensive gold- and silver-wrapped thread that Sally worked throughout—in fact, his own merchant ship may have carried the thread from Europe. The glass-and-wooden frame was an additional expense and sign of wealth.

The choice of a coat of arms also signaled the family's belief in a political philosophy valuing tradition, hierarchy, and obedience to authority. The Peirces, along with many wealthy Salem families, were staunch Federalists. Although they had supported the American colonies' break from Great Britain, Federalists still clung to English ideas about social and political hierarchy. The feudal symbols in Sally's needlework (a shield, escutcheons, and a knight's helmet) refer to a hierarchical system in which the aristocratic few ruled the many, ministers held authority over their congregations, and fathers enjoyed a power unchallenged in the household. Obedience to God, country, and family—not necessarily in that order—was expected from Salem's girls and boys alike, although girls had the added duty of deferring to brothers as well.[242]

On a more personal level, Sally's coat of arms symbolized the end of her childhood as she finished her schooling and looked forward to the next life stage—marriage. Throughout the eighteenth century and well into the nineteenth, female education was intended to be practical training, a method of preparing girls to be good wives, mothers, and household managers. It is true that wealthy women were expected to be better educated than others because a genteel lifestyle demanded additional skills. Girls like Sally learned poetry, Latin, and geography and were given lessons in drawing and dancing.[243] No matter what her station was in life, a woman's job was to marry wealthily, manage wisely, and mother well.

In this light, the Peirce coat of arms seems an ironic choice for Sally's last school project, representing as it did her origins and not her future. A handwritten note on the back confirms that Sally worked the piece for her father before her marriage. Why should she memorialize a family she was preparing to leave? In truth, the needlework reminded Sally and all those around her that regardless of the choices she made—whom she married or how many times she did so—she would carry her family's name and honor with her throughout life. She and any children she had would be Peirces by blood if not by name. It was her duty to bring honor and not shame to her family through her marriage choice.

So this work—a testament to Sally's skill, her teacher's expertise, her father's wealth, her family's status, and her impending marriage—progressed under the watchful eyes of those around her. In September 1797, her elder brother, Benjamin, sent a congratulatory note, having heard good news from a cousin: "George gives me (as it's natural to suppose) a very flattering account of your Arms. However, making allowances for his partiality, I don't hesitate to set them down for beautiful. I congratulate you on your being set at liberty."[244]

Little did Benjamin, Sally, or George know that in a few years the very issue of female liberty would embroil their family in a town scandal that threatened to ruin Sally's teacher and friend, Mrs. Rogers. By the winter of 1800, Sally was no longer a schoolgirl but a young woman, engaged to George Nichols, the same cousin who had admired her needlework. Federalists, like Sally's father, were finding the new century a frightening place as the old social system eroded beneath their feet. George Washington's death in December 1799 signaled the end of one era, while Thomas Jefferson's election to the presidency unveiled

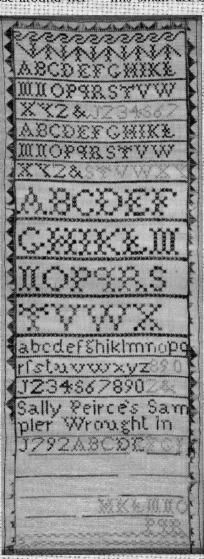

A sampler (1792) by Sally Peirce.

the dawn of a new and uncertain age. Unnerved by the excesses of the French Revolution, Federalists saw radicals, feminists, and atheists lurking in every shadow, threatening to overthrow all church, state, and family authority.

Within this storm of fear and fanaticism, a young woman in Salem staged her own small personal revolt. Sally's cousin, Lydia Nichols, balked at the idea of marrying Benjamin Peirce, Sally's brother. Within a year, this small act of personal resistance triggered a public scandal that reached as far as New Haven, a scandal involving several ministers, three newspapers, and a future United States Supreme Court justice. Before it was over, the public debate touched on ice skating, feminism, religion, and the role of schoolteachers in the new nineteenth century. At the center of the storm, a lightning rod for all this personal and political passion, stood Abigail Rogers, Salem schoolmistress.[245]

The scandal began with Lydia Nichols, described by one descendant as "a high-spirited girl" who grew to be a "very brilliant and able woman."[246] We know little about Lydia's formal education, although family letters reveal that she was able to read Latin and discuss classical poetry with her college-educated male cousin. As an older cousin and confidante of Sally Peirce, Lydia rejoiced when her brother George became engaged to Sally in 1798.[247] She teased Sally's brother Benjamin with this remark: "So you see Cousin we are in a fair way to call each other by & by, by the endearing titles of Brother and Sister."[248]

Lydia and Benjamin's families hoped that by and by the two would call each other by the even closer titles of husband and wife. Benjamin was still a student at Harvard, but his path after graduation was already planned. He was expected to become a merchant like his father and to further cement the Peirce-Nichols connection by marrying Lydia. Sally might be giving up the name of Peirce—the name she had so carefully worked into her father's coat of arms—by marrying George Nichols, but both families expected Lydia Nichols to complete the trade by adding the name of Peirce to her own.

For a while, Lydia seemed happy with the match, exchanging chatty and flirtatious letters with Benjamin during the school year and enjoying his company in Salem during vacations. But during his third year at college, their relationship cooled as he focused more on his studies, even spending his summer vacation at school. Lydia ended their romance in the summer of 1799, triggering a plea from her father to forgive Benjamin for not wooing her more actively. She responded that her mind was made up, and pulled in cousin Sally for support, reporting that Benjamin's own sister "thought I was too easy in letting it alone so long as I have done."[249]

As a free woman at age nineteen, Lydia found her attention soon captured by a new arrival in Salem, a handsome young lawyer named Joseph Story. Only three years out of Harvard, the ambitious Story had already made a name for himself as a poet and orator.[250] He was also quickly developing the reputation of being a "Jacobin" in Federalist Salem. A budding politician and a liberal-thinking Unitarian, Joseph Story rejected aristocratic authority in favor of democracy, prompting Lydia's father to term him "an infidel and a radical."[251]

Joseph and Lydia may have met through Mrs. Rogers, who now taught Joseph's sister in her school. Perhaps they were introduced at a berry-picking or fishing party, both popular social events for Salem's young adults.[252]

Portrait of Joseph Story (1837) by Charles Osgood. Oil on canvas.

144

However it began, the couple met in the late summer of 1800 and were soon spending time together—corresponding through letters, playing cards, and taking drives to Story's home town of Marblehead. Upon Lydia's request, Joseph penned an impromptu poem upon a handkerchief at a party and in private presented her with sentimental verses inscribed on a watchpaper to tuck inside her watch.[253]

In general, Salem elders approved of their children's many social activities, proud they could provide a genteel lifestyle for their family. No doubt they also approved of their sons and daughters meeting eligible marriage partners. Some forms of interaction, however, made parents like Captain Nichols nervous. Soon after Lydia and Joseph met, they and other Salem young people organized coed social clubs. Although the members protested the clubs were innocently "formed with a view of promoting social intercourse," the names they chose for their groups, such as "The Mosquito Fleet," "The Antediluvians," and "Sans Souci," sounded irreverent to their Federalist parents and tinged with the faint aromas of the French Revolution and English anarchism.[254] Lydia and Joseph probably belonged to the same social club, actually called "The Social Group," that was led or chaperoned by their mutual friend, Mrs. Abigail Rogers.[255] If Captain Nichols was nervous about these groups in general, he became truly alarmed when the group's conversation turned to the works of English feminist Mary Wollstonecraft.

In her short but scandalous life, Wollstonecraft had denounced almost every value that good Federalists like Captain Nichols held dear. She argued that society, not biology, kept women in an inferior position within the "tyranny" of marriage. Women, she argued, were capable of attending college, engaging in business, or even running for office.[256] These ideas triggered much discussion in the early 1790s as Americans struggled to define women's place in the new republic. By 1798, Wollstonecraft was dead and her reputation in ruins after her well-intentioned husband, William Godwin, revealed that she had died giving birth to another man's child. By 1800, when Lydia, Joseph, and Mrs. Rogers were discussing her ideas, Mary Wollstonecraft's name was synonymous with adultery, atheism, and immorality. She was certainly not a role model for fine young ladies.[257]

This is not to say that Americans entirely turned their backs on reforming female education. Instead, they absorbed the writings of more moderate thinkers like Englishwoman Hannah More, whose *Strictures on Female Education* appeared in 1799. More agreed that girls needed rigorous schooling, but she argued that women should content themselves with being wives and mothers of male citizens, not try to become citizens

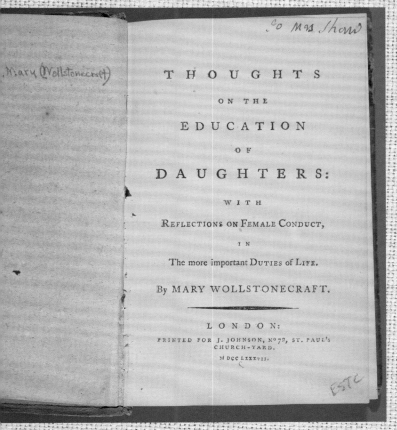

themselves. Benjamin Peirce articulates this approach in a letter to his sister Sally, urging her to continue expanding her mind after completing her embroidery. Although she will never attend Harvard, Sally should read Milton and Pope because "reading is of the utmost importance to discharge rightly the duties of any sphere in life."[258]

More's ideas were so influential in New England that she was saluted in silk embroidery by at least one Salem daughter. Maria Crowninshield was a student in Boston in 1803 when she completed an idealized view of a female academy, complete with a globe and neoclassical drapery (catalogue entry 37). A seated female figure, most likely the teacher, reads aloud from a book by Hannah More, as a pupil stands nearby, absorbing the moral lessons about female modesty and piety.

Lydia Nichols's curiosity about Wollstonecraft's controversial ideas must have concerned her Federalist father.

No doubt the real cause of his alarm was her discussion of these ideas with the "infidel and radical" Joseph Story. Although Story later claimed that he had tried to blend in with Salem society and keep his ideas to himself, Ichabod Nichols caustically remarked to Lydia that "I believe it is very rare that the great are known to talk as much as he does." Concerned that she had become involved with Joseph too soon after breaking off with Benjamin, he urged his daughter not to commit herself too hastily. "In a concern of so much magnitude as that of a Partner for Life," he reminded her that "one false step might make you unhappy to the end of time, and perhaps to eternity."[259] As fall faded into winter, Captain Nichols became increasingly worried that Mary Wollstonecraft and Joseph Story would corrupt Lydia and lead her into an unhappy marriage.

A man of business and maritime commerce, Nichols turned to the family minister, the Reverend Thomas Barnard, for help. Barnard saw grave political and moral danger for Lydia and her friends, and sought to save them through public shaming. He exposed them in a venomous letter printed in the local Federalist newspaper, the *Salem Gazette*, signing it, "A Friend to Her Sex." This letter accused Salem's teenage girls of casting aside the code of obedience to God, country, and family in one fell swoop by agitating for women's rights within their social clubs, which Barnard denounced as "schools where decency and modesty were laid aside." Salem's teenage girls were urged to abandon all Wollstonecraftian ideas, to "throw aside all that un-becoming boldness and profligacy which has hitherto marked their characters, and substitute modesty and piety." The writer's last and only personal attack was saved for Mrs. Abigail Rogers, "the unsex'd director of the Social Group," who was cast as a pied piper, using her "wicked and seductive arts" to lead innocent girls into the river of destruction.[260]

Why was Mrs. Rogers considered such a threat, and how did attacking her prevent Lydia Nichols from marrying Joseph Story? Until this time, Mrs. Rogers had a sterling reputation in Salem and the surrounding towns. In fact, she was among the most respected and highest-paid teachers in Salem and especially renowned for her needlework. One Salem man described her in glowing terms as a "very cultivated lady, of good acquirements, a superior instructor, of great skill and tact in managing her school, and of indomitable energy and perseverance, who gained the love and respect of her pupils."[261]

Another stated that her "steady and firm temper" had brought her "the greatest applause in the education of our daughters, of which she has instructed sixty at one time."[262] Mrs. Rogers attracted pupils from all over the North Shore and seemed skilled at walking the line between Federalists and their opponents. At her school, daughters from both sides mixed, and "many ties of friendship were thus formed between families estranged by the asperities of politics 'Federal and Jacobin,' running at that period extremely high."[263]

Still, Abigail Rogers stood out from her peers in significant ways, making her a lightning rod in the charged atmosphere of debates about politics, religion, morality, and philosophy. To begin with, she was a constant reminder to concerned parents like Captain Nichols that a poor marriage choice could haunt a woman for the rest of her life. Born in 1764 into a well-to-do Ipswich family, Abigail Dodge had herself received "the best education of our New England families" at a Newburyport boarding school.[264] In return, she was expected to marry a man who met her parents' approval. Instead, at age twenty-one, she willfully attached herself to Nathaniel Rogers, an Ipswich tradesman one year her elder. A good prospect on paper—a Harvard graduate descended from a prominent local family—Nathaniel failed to impress her parents in person. When the couple married in 1784, her parents refused to give a dowry and disowned her. Any hopes of economic or emotional reconciliation were dashed two years later when her father died in debt. Four years after their marriage, Nathaniel, Abigail, and their three young sons moved to Salem for a fresh start.

Trouble followed them there as well, and it soon became clear that Abigail had married a man chronically incapable of providing for his family. Nathaniel's choice of teaching as a profession had more to do with defeat than desire. Several times, he tried to establish himself as a merchant, in Ipswich and later in Salem, but each time the business failed. He fell back on his college degree that virtually assured him of a job as a teacher, although it could not ensure his conduct. In January of 1797, the Salem school committee voted to dismiss Rogers from his position as master of the grammar school after he "behaved so much out of character" that "the public discontents have really become great."[265]

When Nathaniel died mysteriously in 1799 some sixty miles north on the Maine frontier, his thirty-five-year-old widow Abigail was left with four sons to raise on an estate worth only seventy-five dollars and consisting mainly of furniture but no real property.[266] On her own, she became the breadwinner that Nathaniel never was, and her success as an independent and financially savvy business operator challenged the established role of women in society.

Mrs. Rogers left no direct evidence of her political leanings, but letters in her defense suggest that she, like Joseph Story, had more liberal leanings than most of her Salem neighbors. By February of 1801, the issue had expanded from a local controversy to a regional scandal after a powerful Federalist paper in Boston, the *Columbian Centinel*, reprinted Reverend Barnard's letter.[267] Soon the friends of Mrs. Rogers were writing their own letters to defend her reputation as "a respectable private character . . . arraigned before so public a tribunal." At times, this support only added more fuel to the fire. One vociferous supporter began well by asking a rhetorical question: "Has she offended by her noble exertions to support her family, and save them from ruin amidst the most distressing circumstances?" The writer also confirmed that she had "dared to think for herself" on the topic of religion. It was also asserted that she had "adopted Wollstonecraftian principles."[268]

By March of 1801, nearly every issue of the *Gazette*, *Columbian Centinel*, and *Salem Impartial Register* carried a vicious attack or counterattack on the topic of women's rights, Wollstonecraft, Mrs. Rogers, and her defenders. The public controversy took a heavy toll on the schoolteacher's health. Friends worried she would break either financially or physically under the strain, while her doctor admitted to Lydia that the teacher's condition was "alarming and only greatest care of her self alone can restore her."[269] Her minister, William Bentley, visited Mrs. Rogers's school, recording in his diary that she was "suffering from the base invectives of a writer in the *Salem Gazette* whose name cannot be obtained. It may cost her her life."[270]

The romantic relationship between Lydia and Joseph was also suffering that spring. Joseph had proved one of the staunchest supporters of Mrs. Rogers, writing letter after letter to the papers in her defense, signing himself "One of Many." Having attended a coeducational school in his youth, Story firmly agreed with Wollstonecraft that women could become men's intellectual equals if only given the chance.[271] No doubt, he also wanted to defend the reputations of Salem's young women, especially Lydia, but the young, impetuous lawyer was so enraged by the scandal that he made a tactical error by exposing his real identity in a bumbling 5 March letter to the *Centinel*. This opened him up to personal ridicule because none of the other writers ever stepped out from behind their protective pseudonyms. Joseph stood alone, looking even more ridiculous when he challenged the anonymous Boston columnist to a duel.

Around this time, Lydia broke off their relationship, triggering a remarkably poignant letter from Joseph. Calling himself "your friend—your lover—your betrothed partner," Joseph struggled to contain his emotions, even laying down his pen at one point until he had better control. Recognizing it was natural for Captain Nichols's "parental solicitude" to prefer her cousin Benjamin as a son-in-law, Joseph argued that the final decision belonged to Lydia: "you ought as a duty to heaven, to yourself, and to me to quench every attempt at controlling the liberal election of your heart." Chafing against Federalist principles, Joseph insisted that he and Lydia were "bound to each other by irremovable ties—ties which neither time nor fate nor authority can dissolve." These ties had been spoken by their hearts, seconded by the angels, and "ratified" by their lips. His rants against the "doctrine of subjugation" and "infallibility of parental authority" slowly gave way to expressions of the grief, despair, and drama that come most intensely to young lovers. The letter ends with this prediction, "unless my mind is more at rest—I shall soon love you only in the grave."[272]

Of course, neither Joseph, Mrs. Rogers, nor Lydia died from the effects of the scandal. By the summer of 1801, the storm had passed, and Mrs. Rogers continued to draw students from local families on both sides of the political divide. Three years later, Joseph married another woman, who died shortly thereafter. His second wife presented him with seven children and saw him rise far above the expectations of Lydia's father. Joseph Story became a United States congressman, a speaker of the Massachusetts House of Representatives, and a justice of the United States Supreme Court. He returned to Harvard as a popular professor of law.[273]

Lydia Nichols eventually renewed her affections for her cousin Benjamin Peirce, who graduated from Harvard College in 1801 and returned home to join the family business. The two married in 1803, two years after their siblings Sally Peirce and George Nichols. When Benjamin's business failed under the restrictions of President Jefferson's trade embargo, he moved his family to Cambridge and became an influential librarian at Harvard. The two former rivals, Benjamin Peirce and Joseph Story, ended as neighbors, corresponding dispassionately about how to obtain old copies of the *Columbian Centinel* for the school's library.[274] Benjamin died at age 53 in 1831 of a sudden brain fever.[275]

Abigail Dodge Rogers herself died at 53 in 1817, of St. Anthony's fire (erysipelas). Reverend Bentley recorded her death along with a note that she "in adverse circumstances came to Salem, was a distinguished school-mistress and educated her children well."[276] Her old attacker, the *Columbian Centinel*, had no comment on her passing but printed a brief death notice two days later.[277] She had lived to see one of her sons become a successful artist and another a prominent businessman.

As a postscript, the most unusual accusation against the beleaguered Mrs. Rogers came several months after things had cooled down. In the fall of 1801, Federalist Benjamin Silliman began attacking the moral degeneration of his age in a book that purported to be a series of letters from a Hindu traveler named Shahcoolen to a friend in India. Among his many assaults on Mary Wollstonecraft was one report that a Salem woman "initiates young virgins, into the invigorating exercise of [ice] skating." His chief concern was "that the narrow apparel of fashionable females, would greatly impede the exertions of the fair one's energies, in this most slippery diversion; and should she fall headlong, (an accident which often occurs to boys,) who can divine the consequences, which might ensue?"[278]

Fortunately, Salem's school for scandal had lost the public's interest, even as Joseph Story had lost Lydia Nichols's heart. A lone letter to the *Salem Register* gave the final word on the controversy in general, charging that the "absolute falsehood," came from a "silly writer [who] only intended to wound the innocent." The wise writer asked all to consider "what can we conclude from such papers, unless they are vehicles of Scandal, and deserving of neglect and contempt."[279]

1. Lloyd E. Herman, foreword to *Celebrating the Stitch: Contemporary Embroidery of North America*, by Barbara Lee Smith (Newtown, Conn.: Taunton Press, 1991), viii.

2. Sandra Dennis, "Schoolgirl Embroidery, Grown-Up Prices," *Business Week*, 17 March 1997.

3. The HIA [Hobby Industry Association] 1998 Nationwide Craft/Hobby Consumer Study reported that "the various needlecraft-related activities continue to be the crafts with the most widespread participation"; available from the HIA Internet web site <http://www.hobby.org/chcs98.html>.

4. Barbara Lee Smith, *Celebrating the Stitch: Contemporary Embroidery of North America* (Newtown, Conn.: Taunton Press, 1991); Nancy Orban, ed., *Fiberarts Design Book Six* (Ashville, N.C.: Lark Books, 1999); and Anne Morrell, *Contemporary Embroidery: Exciting and Innovative Textile Art* (London: Studio Vista, 1994).

5. *Catalogue of Antique Articles on Exhibition at Plummer Hall, Salem, December 1875 and Supplement* (Salem, Mass.: Press of the *Salem Gazette* for the Ladies' Centennial Committee, 1875).

6. *Salem at the World's Columbian Exposition, Chicago, 1893* (Salem, Mass.: Essex Institute, 1893), 47–48.

7. Sarah Anna Emery, *Reminiscences of a Nonagenarian* (Newburyport, Mass.: William H. Huse, 1879), 222.

8. Betty Ring, *Let Virtue Be a Guide to Thee: Needlework in the Education of Rhode Island Women, 1730–1830* (Providence: Rhode Island Historical Society, 1983), 32–33; and Ethel Stanwood Bolton and Eva Johnston Coe, *American Samplers* (New York: Dover Publications, 1921), iv, 5, 9.

9. Carol Humphrey, *Samplers: Fitzwilliam Museum Handbook* (Cambridge, England: Cambridge University Press, 1997), 36–43; Kathleen Epstein, *British Embroidery: Curious Works from the Seventeenth Century* (Austin, Tex.: Curious Works Press for the Colonial Williamsburg Foundation, 1998), 10–16; and Clare Browne and Jennifer Wearden, *Samplers from the Victoria and Albert Museum* (London: Victoria and Albert Museum, 2000), 7–9, 46–51.

10. Robert Charles Anderson, *The Great Migration Begins: Immigrants to New England, 1620–1633* (Boston: Great Migration Study Project, New England Historic Genealogical Society, 1995), 639–46; and *Sketches about Salem People* (Salem, Mass.: The Club, 1930), 5, 13.

11. *Salem at the World's Columbian Exposition*, 47.

12. Xanthe Brooke, *The Lady Lever Art Gallery Catalogue of Embroideries* (Wolfeboro, N.H.: Allen Sutton Publishing for the Trustees of the National Museums and Galleries on Merseyside, 1992), 247; and Jane Ashelford, *The Art of Dress: Clothes and Society, 1500–1914* (New York: Harry N. Abrams, 1996), 77–79.

13. Henry Wilder Foote, comp., *Catalogue of Portraits in the Essex Institute, Salem, Massachusetts* (Salem: Essex Institute, 1936), 117; and John Howland to the Essex Historical Society, 2 December 1822, American Decorative Arts Department files, Peabody Essex Museum.

14. Patricia Trautman, "Dress in Seventeenth-Century Cambridge, Massachusetts: An Inventory-Based Reconstruction," in *Early American Probate Inventories* (Boston: Boston University Press, 1989), 52–55.

15. Santina M. Levey, "English Embroidered Cabinets of the Seventeenth Century," *Antiques* 139 (1991): 1130–39; and Margaret Swain, *Embroidered Stuart Pictures* (Princes Risborough, Buckinghamshire, England: Shire Publications, 1991), 9–10.

16. Betty Ring, *Girlhood Embroidery: American Samplers and Pictorial Needlework, 1650–1850* (New York: Alfred A. Knopf, 1993), 31–35; and Levey, "English Embroidered Cabinets of the Seventeenth Century," 1138–39.

17. Levey, "English Embroidered Cabinets of the Seventeenth Century," 1139.

18. Epstein, *British Embroidery*, 17–19; and Brooke, *The Lady Lever Art Gallery Catalogue of Embroideries*, 15–16, 53–54.

19. Kathleen Epstein, conversation with Paula Richter, 20 June 1991.

20. *Catalogue of Antique Articles on Exhibition at Plummer Hall, Salem.*

21. Ring, *Girlhood Embroidery*, 29; Humphrey, *Samplers: Fitzwilliam Museum Handbook*, 16, 22; Jonathan L. Fairbanks and Robert F. Trent, *New England Begins: The Seventeenth Century* (Boston: Museum of Fine Arts, 1982), 403–4; Nicola J. Shilliam, "The Needle's Excellency: English Needlework of the Tudor and Stuart Periods in the Museum of Fine Arts, Boston," *Antiques* 149 (1996): 850–61; and Bolton and Coe, *American Samplers*, xiii, 5.

22. George F. Chever, "A Sketch of Philip English—A Merchant in Salem from about 1670 to about 1733–4," *Essex Institute Historical Collections* 1 (1859): 159; Mrs. N. S. Bell, comp., *Pathways of the Puritans* (Framingham, Mass.: Old America Publishers, 1930), 204–5; and Henry W. Belknap, "Philip English, Commerce Builder," *Proceedings of the American Antiquarian Society* 41 (1931): 17–24.

23. *The Diary of the Reverend William Bentley, D.D.* (1911; reprint, Gloucester, Mass.: Peter Smith, 1962), 2:23–26.

24. Nancy Graves Cabot, "The Fishing Lady and Boston Common," *Antiques* 40 (1941): 28–31; Nancy Graves Cabot, "Engravings and Embroideries: The Sources of Some Designs in the Fishing Lady Pictures," *Antiques* 40 (1941): 367–69; Ring, *Girlhood Embroidery*, 44–59; Brooke, *The Lady Lever Art Gallery Catalogue of Embroideries*, 93–97; Margaret Swain, *Embroidered Georgian Pictures* (Princes Risborough, Buckinghamshire, England: Shire Publications, 1994), 7–9; and Thomasina Beck, *Gardening with Silk and Gold: A History of Gardens in Embroidery* (Newton Abbot, Devon, England: David and Charles, 1997), 85–91.

25. Elizabeth Carroll Reilly, *A Dictionary of Colonial American Printers' Ornaments and Illustrations* (Worcester, Mass.: American Antiquarian Society, 1975), 421; and A. Hyatt Mayor, "The Hunt for the Fishing Lady," *Antiques* 112 (1977): 113.

26. *Diary of the Reverend William Bentley*, 1:162; and museum accession records, American Decorative Arts Department files, Peabody Essex Museum.

27. Ring, *Girlhood Embroidery*, 36; and Joan Stephens to Anne Farnam, 4 September 1987, American Decorative Arts Department files. Related samplers with the "Spies of Canaan" motif include the one worked by Sarah Courtis in 1770 (acc. no. 109644) and by Hannah Safford in 1787 (acc. no. 129086).

28. Susan Burrows Swan, *Plain and Fancy: American Women and Their Needlework, 1650–1850* (Austin, Tex.: Curious Works Press, 1995), 52–55.

29. *Sibley's Harvard Graduates* (Boston, Mass.: Massachusetts Historical Society, 1960), 11:322–25; and Waldo Lincoln, comp., *Genealogy of the Waldo Family* (Worcester, Mass.: Charles Hamellan, 1902), 183–91.

30. Rozsika Parker, *The Subversive Stitch: Embroidery and the Making of the Feminine* (New York: Routledge, 1989), 112–16; and Beck, *Gardening with Silk and Gold*, 85–91.

31. Ashelford, *The Art of Dress*, 122–24, 128.

32. Carrie Rebora et al., *John Singleton Copley in America* (New York: Metropolitan Museum of Art, 1995).

33. Ashelford, *The Art of Dress*, 122–27; Gervase Jackson-Stops and James Pipkin, *The English Country House: A Grand Tour* (Boston: Little, Brown, 1985), 42–43; Parker, *The Subversive Stitch*, 111–18; Ring, *Girlhood Embroidery*, 44–53; and Beck, *Gardening with Silk and Gold*, 85–91.

34. Geneva A. Daland and James S. Mansfield, comp., *Mansfield Genealogy* (Portsmouth, N.H.: Peter Randall, 1980), 48–49; James Duncan Phillips, *Salem in the Eighteenth Century* (New York: Houghton Mifflin, 1937), 336; Ethel Hall Bjerkoe, *The Cabinetmakers of America* (Exton, Penn.: Schiffer, 1957), 226; and additional provenance information on file in the American Decorative Arts Department, Peabody Essex Museum.

35. Ring, *Girlhood Embroidery*, 44–53; Helen Bowen, "The Fishing Lady and Boston Common," *Antiques* (1923): 70–73; Cabot, "The Fishing Lady and Boston Common," 28–31; and Cabot, "Engravings and Embroideries," 367–69.

36. Parker, *The Subversive Stitch*, 116–17; and Beck, *Gardening with Silk and Gold*, 85–91.

37. Margaret T. J. Rowe, *Exhibition of Crewel Work Found in New England Held at Gore Place, Waltham, Massachusetts* (Waltham, Mass.: Gore Place, 1963), 20–21.

38. Ashelford, *The Art of Dress*, 122; and *Michele Felice Cornè, Versatile Neapolitan Painter* (Salem, Mass.: Peabody Museum of Salem, 1962), 21, figs. 45, 47.

39. Ring, *Girlhood Embroidery*, 45–53, 100–102; and Cabot, "The Fishing Lady and Boston Common," 28.

40. Glee Krueger, *New England Samplers to 1840* (Sturbridge, Mass.: Old Sturbridge Village, 1978), 16–18, fig. 23.

41. "Salem Baptisms," *Essex Institute Historical Collections* 23 (1889): 8; "List of Salem Vessels Insured by Timothy Orne, John Nutting, Jr. and John Higgenson," *Essex Institute Historical Collections* 37 (1903): 79; *Essex Institute Historical Collections* 69 (1935): 49, 53.

42. "Diary of Mrs. Mary (Vial) Holyoke," *The Holyoke Diaries, 1709–1856* (Salem, Mass.: Essex Institute, 1911), 67.

43. Dean Lahikainen, *In the American Spirit: Folk Art from the Collections* (Salem, Mass.: Peabody Essex Museum, 1994), 17.

44. Abbott Lowell Cummings, *Bed Hangings: A Treatise on Fabrics and Styles in the Curtaining of Beds, 1650–1850* (Boston, Mass.: Society for the Preservation of New England Antiquities, 1994), 1–138; Florence Montgomery, "18th Century American Bed and Window Hangings," in Edward S. Cooke Jr., ed., *Upholstery in America and Europe from the Seventeenth Century to World War I* (New York: W. W. Norton, 1987), 163–73; and Swan, *Plain and Fancy*, 121–24.

45. Cummings, *Bed Hangings*, 37–38; and Rowe, *Exhibition of Crewel Work Found in New England Held at Gore Place*, 14, item 31.

46. Ann Pollard Rowe, "Crewel Embroidered Bedhangings in Old and New England," *Bulletin of the Museum of Fine Arts, Boston* 71 (1973), 144–49; and Beck, *Gardening with Silk and Gold*, 80–84.

47. Mildred J. Davis, *The Art of Crewel Embroidery* (New York: Crown Publishers, 1962), 19–48; and Mary Taylor Landon and Susan Burrows Swan, *American Crewel Work* (London: MacMillan, 1970), 24–25.

48. Jonathan B. Butcher, "The Eveleth Family of Colonial New England," *New England Historical and Genealogical Register* 134 (1980): 299–309; and *New England Historical and Genealogical Register* 135 (1981): 23–35.

49. *Portraits of Shipmasters and Merchants in the Peabody Museum of Salem* (Salem: Peabody Museum of Salem, 1939), 37–38; Russell Leigh Jackson, comp., *Additions to the Catalogue of Portraits in the Essex Institute* (Salem, Mass.: Essex Institute, 1950), 14–16; Charles Osgood and H. M. Batchelder, *Historical Sketch of Salem* (Salem: Essex Institute, 1879), 130–32; and Perley Derby, "Genealogy of the Derby Family," *Essex Institute Historical Collections* 3 (1861): 161, 201–3.

50. Wendy A. Cooper, "Nathaniel and Elizabeth West and the Ownership of the Farm at Danvers," *Museum of Fine Arts Bulletin* 81 (1983): 15–23; Wendy A. Cooper, "The Furniture and Furnishings of the Farm at Danvers," *Museum of Fine Arts Bulletin* 81 (1983): 24–45; and *Diary of the Reverend William Bentley*, 3:260–62, 4:240–41.

51. George Ferguson, *Signs and Symbols in Christian Art* (New York: Oxford University Press, 1976), 23, 37; and *Emblems for the Improvement and Entertainment of Youth* (London: R. Ware, 1755), 37, 45–46.

52. Patricia E. Kane, *Colonial Massachusetts Silversmiths and Jewelers* (New Haven: Yale University Art Gallery, 1998), 552.

53. Ring, *Girlhood Embroidery*, 40–41, 50–53.

54. Miniature portraits of the Foster family are in the American Decorative Arts Department of the Peabody Essex Museum (127941, 127942, and 127944).

55. Ring, *Girlhood Embroidery*, 105–7; Bolton and Coe, *American Samplers*, plate 90, 364; Swan, *Plain and Fancy*, 66; and Mary Jane Edmonds, *Samplers and Samplermakers: An American Schoolgirl Art, 1700–1850* (New York: Rizzoli for the Los Angeles County Museum of Art, 1991), 30–33.

56. Paula Bradstreet Richter, "Samplers from Mistress Sarah Stivours School, Salem, Massachusetts," *PieceWork* 8 (2000): 28–33.

57. Isaac Watts, *Horae Lyricae: Poems Chiefly of the Lyric Kind* (Boston: Daniel Kneeland for Nicholas Bowes, 1772), 10.

58. Richter, "Samplers from Mistress Sarah Stivours School," 28–33.

59. Alan I. Ludwig, *Graven Images: New England Stonecarving and Its Symbols, 1650–1815* (Middletown, Conn.: Wesleyan University Press, 1966), 14–16.

60. Ring, *Girlhood Embroidery*, 106, 108; Krueger, *New England Samplers to 1840*, 16, fig. 24; and Lahikainen, *In the American Spirit*, 18, 55.

61. *Portraits of Shipmasters and Merchants*, 128, 129; and Katherine A. Harrigan, "Schoolgirl Samplers of Federal Salem, Massachusetts, 1783–1820" (master's thesis, Cooper-Hewitt Museum and the Parsons School of Design, 1995), 55–56.

62. Ring, *Girlhood Embroidery*, 60–74.

63. Betty Ring, "Heraldic Embroidery in Eighteenth-Century Boston," *Antiques* 141 (1992): 622–31.

64. Frederick Clifton Pierce, *Fiske and Fisk Family* (Chicago, 1896), 102–4.

65. *Diary of the Reverend William Bentley*, 1:22, 176.

66. Ring, *Girlhood Embroidery*, 105–7; Edmonds, *Samplers and Samplermakers*, 30–31; and Richter, "Samplers from Mistress Sarah Stivours School," 28–33.

67. Bolton and Coe, *American Samplers*, 271.

68. Bjerkoe, *The Cabinetmakers of America*, 188–89; and Foote, *Catalogue of Portraits in the Essex Institute*, 45–46.

69. Ashelford, *The Art of Dress*, 135–40; Jean L. Druesedow, *In Style: Celebrating Fifty Years of the Costume Institute* (New York: Metropolitan Museum of Art, 1987), 22–23; Jean Starobinski et al., *Revolution in Fashion: European Clothing, 1715–1815* (New York: Abbeville Press, 1989), 71, 111, 144, 146; Anne Hollander, *Sex and Suits* (New York: Kodansha International, 1995), 83–84; and Charles Germain de Saint-Aubin, *Art of the Embroiderer*, translated by Nikki Scheuer and notes by Edward Maeder (Boston: Los Angeles County Museum in association with David R. Godine, 1983).

70. Peter W. Cook, "Cockfighting in North America and New England, 1680–1900," in *New England's Creatures: 1400–1900* (Boston: Boston University for the Dublin Seminar for New England Folklife, 1995), 164–82; Jacques Anquetil, *Silk* (New York: Flammarion, 1995), 114–15; and Beck, *Gardening with Silk and Gold*, 5.

71. Benjamin Peirce to Sarah Peirce, September 1797, Nichols Family Papers, Phillips Library, Peabody Essex Museum.

72. Ring, *Girlhood Embroidery*, 272.

73. Gerald W. R. Ward, *The Peirce-Nichols House* (Salem, Mass.: Essex Institute, 1976).

74. Nathaniel Rogers's General Store and School Account Book: General Store, Ipswich, 1783 and Schoolmaster, Salem, 1789–1794, Rogers Family Papers, Phillips Library, Peabody Essex Museum; and Harrigan, "Schoolgirl Samplers of Federal Salem," 83–84.

75. Reward of Merit for Miss Eliza Peirce from the Rogers school, ca. 1800, Phillips Library, Peabody Essex Museum.

76. Betty Ring, "New England Heraldic Needlework of the Neoclassical Period," *Antiques* 144 (1993): 485.

77. *Diary of the Reverend William Bentley*, 2:441.

78. Benjamin Peirce to Sarah Peirce, September 1797, Nichols Family Papers, Phillips Library, Peabody Essex Museum; and Ring, *Girlhood Embroidery*, 107.

79. Susan Nichols Pulsifer, *Witches' Breed: The Peirce-Nichols Family of Salem* (Cambridge, Mass.: Dresser, Chapman and Grimes, 1967), 62, 381–82.

80. Dan L. Monroe et al., *Gifts of the Spirit: Works by Nineteenth-Century and Contemporary Native American Artists* (Salem, Mass.: Peabody Essex Museum, 1996), 10–18.

81. Ruth Phillips, *Trading Identities: The Souvenir in Native North American Art from the Northeast, 1700–1900* (Seattle: University of Washington Press, 1998), 250–54; Meredith Wright, *Put on Thy Beautiful Garments: Rural New England Clothing, 1783–1800* (East Montpelier, Vt.: The Clothes Press, 1990), 14, 86; David-Thiery Ruddel, "Clothing, Society, and Consumer Trends in the Montreal Area, 1792–1835," in *New England/New France, 1000–1850* (Boston: Boston University Press for the Dublin Seminar for New England Folklife, 1992), 130; and Nancy E. Rexford, *Women's Shoes in America, 1795–1930* (Kent, Ohio: Kent State University Press, 2000), plate 13, 99, 151.

82. Phillips, *Trading Identities*, 250–54.

83. Ring, *Girlhood Embroidery*, 131–43.

84. Ibid., 143.

85. Davida Tenenbaum Deutsch and Betty Ring, "Homage to Washington in Needlework and Prints," *Antiques* 119 (1981): 402.

86. Wendy C. Wick, *George Washington, An American Icon: The Eighteenth-Century Graphic Portraits* (Washington, D.C.: Barra Foundation Book in conjunction with the Smithsonian Institution Traveling Exhibition Service and the National Portrait Gallery, 1982), 70–71.

87. Deutsch and Ring, "Homage to Washington in Needlework and Prints," 418. Related imagery appeared in a schoolgirl watercolor by Charlotte Chandler Tenney at the Bradford Academy of Bradford, Massachusetts, "Droit de l'homme et du citoyen," ca. 1833. See John Hardy Wright, *Vernacular Visions: Folk Art of Old Newbury* (Newburyport, Mass.: Historical Society of Old Newbury, 1994), 40.

88. Georgiana Brown Harbeson, *American Needlework* (New York: Bonanza Books, 1938), 88; and Swain, *Embroidered Georgian Pictures*, 29.

89. Salem, Massachusetts, vital records; and G. Andrews, "The Carleton Family of Salem," *Essex Institute Historical Collections* 86 (1950): 146, 147.

90. Emery, *Reminiscences of a Nonagenarian*, 223.

91. Parker, *The Subversive Stitch*, 138–39.

92. Ring, *Let Virtue Be a Guide to Thee*, 101, 198–200.

93. Jane C. Nylander, "Some Print Sources of New England Schoolgirl Art," *Antiques* 110 (1976): 296–97; and Corinna Lotz, "Angelika Kauffmann," *Apollo* 149 (1999): 59–60.

94. Ring, *Girlhood Embroidery*, 80.

95. Ring, *Girlhood Embroidery*, 20–22; and Swan, *Plain and Fancy*, 197–201.

96. Deutsch and Ring, "Homage to Washington in Needlework and Prints," 415.

97. Peter Benes, *Old-Town and the Waterside: Two Hundred Years of Tradition and Change in Newbury, Newburyport, and West Newbury, 1635–1835* (Newburyport, Mass.: Historical Society of Old Newbury, 1986), 13.

98. Ring, *Girlhood Embroidery*, 114–23; Benes, *Old-Town and the Waterside*, 68–69, 174–75; and Wright, *Vernacular Visions*, 34–35.

99. Leonard Allison Morrison and Stephen Paschall Sharples, *History of the Kimball Family in America from 1634 to 1897* (1897; reprint, Interlaken, N.Y.: Heart of the Lakes Publishing, 1981), 227; Ebenezer Alden, M.D., *Memorial of the Descendants of the Hon. John Alden* (Randolph, Mass.: Samuel P. Brown, 1867), 84; Rev. Increase N. Tarbox, "Ebenezer Alden, M.D.," *New England Historical and Genealogical Register* 35 (1881): 312–14; and Myron O. Allen, M.D., *History of Wenham* (1860; reprint, Wenham, Mass.: Wenham Historical Association and Museum, 1975), 139–40.

100. Maria Crowninshield to Hannah Crowninshield, 20 August 1804, Crowninshield Family Papers, Phillips Library, Peabody Essex Museum.

101. Ring, *Girlhood Embroidery*, 94–99; and Betty Ring, "Mrs. Saunders' and Miss Beach's Academy, Dorchester," *Antiques* 110 (1976): 302–12.

102. Hannah More, *Strictures on the Modern System of Female Education with a View of the Principles and Conduct Prevalent among Women of Rank and Fortune* (Salem, Mass.: Samuel West, 1809); Parker, *The Subversive Stitch*, 139–43; and Swan, *Plain and Fancy*, 175–84.

103. Sarah Wagner-Wright, "Genealogy of the Crowninshield Family," manuscript in the collections of the Phillips Library, Peabody Essex Museum; and *Diary of the Reverend William Bentley*, 4:247.

104. Bolton and Coe, *American Samplers*, 132.

105. L. Vernon Briggs, *History and Genealogy of the Briggs Family, 1254–1937* (Boston: Charles E. Goodspeed, 1938), 402; and Foote, *Catalogue of Portraits in the Essex Institute*, 249–50.

106. Ring, *Girlhood Embroidery*, 94–99; Ring, "Mrs. Saunders' and Miss Beach's Academy, Dorchester," 302–12; and *The Joan Stephens Collection*, Sotheby's, sale 6,942, 19 January 1997, lot 2,015.

107. Nylander, "Some Print Sources of New England Schoolgirl Art," 296–97.

108. Ring, *Girlhood Embroidery*, 98.

109. Ring, *Girlhood Embroidery*, 114–29, 232–35; and Elisabeth Donaghy Garrett, "Canterbury Tales: Notes on a New Hampshire School of Needlework," in *Lessons Stitched in Silk: Samplers from the Canterbury Region of New Hampshire* (Hanover, N.H.: Trustees of Dartmouth College, 1990), 6–7.

110. Rowley vital records; "Marriage Records of the Rev. Thomas Baldwin, Pastor of the Second Baptist Church, Boston, Massachusetts," *New England Historical and Genealogical Register* 126 (1972): 141, 143.

111. Beck, *Gardening with Silk and Gold*, 80–99; Harbeson, *American Needlework*, 89; and Swan, *Plain and Fancy*, 184–86.

112. Parker, *The Subversive Stitch*, 119–23.

113. George Francis Chever, genealogical notebooks, Chever Family Papers, 1816–59, Phillips Library, Peabody Essex Museum; and Eldridge Goss, *History of Melrose* (Melrose, Mass.: City of Melrose, 1902), 127, 349.

114. Oliver Goldsmith, *The Deserted Village* (Springfield, Mass.: Babcock and Haswell, 1783), 314.

115. Anne Farnam, "Textiles at the Essex Institute," *Essex Institute Historical Collections* 110 (1974): figs. 6, 7.

116. *Memoir Biographical and Genealogical of Sir John Leverett, Knt.* (Boston: Crosby, Nichols, 1856), 160; and Lahikainen, *In the American Spirit*, 24.

117. Krueger, *New England Samplers to 1840*, 181; Louise Hall Tharp, *The Peabody Sisters of Salem* (Boston: Little, Brown, 1988), 21; and Harbeson, *American Needlework*, 90.

118. American Decorative Arts Department files, 100513.

119. Nylander, "Some Print Sources of New England Schoolgirl Art," 294–96.

120. "Salem's Famous Family," *Boston Globe*, 23 September 1903.

121. Nancy Goyne Evans, *American Windsor Furniture: Specialized Forms* (New York: Hudson Hills Press in association with the Henry Francis du Pont Winterthur Museum, 1997), 201–4.

122. Lahikainen, *In the American Spirit*, 24, 87; and Jane C. Nylander, "Country Rugs," *Antiques* 144 (1993): 524–26.

123. Emery, *Reminiscences of a Nonagenarian*, 222–23.

124. Cynthia V. A. Schaffner and Susan Klein, *American Painted Furniture, 1790–1880* (New York: Clarkson Potter Publishers, 1997), 29–31.

125. Lahikainen, *In the American Spirit*, 23.

126. Charles F. Montgomery, *American Furniture: The Federal Period, in the Henry Francis du Pont Winterthur Museum* (New York: Viking Press, 1966), figs. 478 and 481; Dean A. Fales Jr., *American Painted Furniture, 1660–1880* (New York: Bonanza Books, 1986), 177–83; Schaffner and Klein, *American Painted Furniture*, 29–31; and Wright, *Vernacular Visions*, 64, 65.

127. Lahikainen, *In the American Spirit*, 23.

128. Mr. Cole's Female School, List of Scholars [1807–34], 1, 2. Essex County Collection, Private Schools, Phillips Library, Peabody Essex Museum.

129. Joseph B. Felt, *Annals of Salem* (Salem, Mass.: W. and S. B. Ives, 1845), 462.

130. Eliza Whittredge's sampler (137581.143) and embroidered picture (130551) are in the collections of the American Decorative Arts Department, Peabody Essex Museum.

131. Foote, *Catalogue of Portraits in the Essex Institute*, 45–46.

132. Vital records of Salem, Massachusetts, 1:228, 5:201.

133. Mr. Cole's Female School, List of Scholars [1807–34], 5, 6.

134. Anne Farnam, "Olive Prescott, Weaver of Forge Village," *Essex Institute Historical Collections* 115 (1979): 129–43; Martha Coons with Katherine Koob, *All Sorts of Good Sufficient Cloth: Linen-Making in New England, 1640–1860* (North Andover, Mass., 1980), 114; and William Prescott, M.D., *The Prescott Memorial; or, A Genealogical Memoir of the Prescott Families in America* (Boston: Henry W. Dutton and Son, 1870), 102, 144.

135. Stella Blum, ed., *Ackermann's Costume Plates: Women's Fashions in England, 1818–1828* (New York: Dover Publications, 1978), vi; and Harbeson, *American Needlework*, 147.

136. J. Wesley Hanson, *Flora's Dial: Containing a Flower Dedicated to Each Day in the Year* (Lowell, Mass.: Jonathan Allen, 1846), 181; Mary M. Griffin, *Drops from Flora's Cup; or, The Poetry of Flowers, with a Floral Vocabulary* (Boston: Oliver L. Perkins, 1846), 154; and *The Bouquet: Containing the Poetry and Language of Flowers* (Boston: Benjamin B. Mussey, 1846).

137. Swan, *Plain and Fancy*, 160–61, 231–32, 240; and Patricia T. Herr, "The Ornamental Branches": Needlework and Arts from the *Lititz Moravian Girls' School between 1800 and 1965* (Lancaster, Penn.: Heritage Center Museum of Lancaster County, 1996), 46–47.

138. Miss Lambert, *The Hand-Book of Needlework* (New York: Wiley and Putnam, 1842), 65–66, 69.

139. Judith Walsh, "The Language of Flowers in Nineteenth-Century American Painting," *Antiques* 156 (1999): 518–31; Griffin, *Drops from Flora's Cup*, 158; and *The Bouquet*, 103, 128.

140. Harbeson, *American Needlework*, 147; C. Willett Cunnington, *English Women's Clothing in the Nineteenth Century* (New York: Dover Publications, 1990), 115.

141. J. Welles Henderson and Rodney P. Carlisle, *Marine Art and Antiques, Jack Tar: A Sailor's Life, 1750–1910* (Woodbridge, Suffolk, England: Antique Collectors' Club, 1999), 50–53, 107–113; and Mark Isaksen, *Woolies: Embroidered Ship Portraits* (Philadelphia: Philadelphia Maritime Museum, 1993).

142. Nicholas Thomas, *Oceanic Art* (London: Thames and Hudson, 1995), 99–114; and Henderson and Carlisle, *Marine Art and Antiques*, 258–62.

143. William Sargent et al., *Views of the Pearl River Delta: Macao, Canton, and Hong Kong* (Hong Kong: Urban Council of Hong Kong, 1996), 76; Carl Crossman, *The China Trade* (Woodbridge, Suffolk, England: Antique Collectors' Club, 1991), 269, 273; and Nerylla Taunton, *Antique Needlework Tools and Embroideries* (Woodbridge, Suffolk, England: Antique Collectors' Club, 1997), 117–18, 106–7.

144. John A. Cherol, "Chateau-sur-Mer in Newport, Rhode Island," in Elisabeth Donaghy Garrett, *The Antiques Book of Victorian Interiors* (New York: Crown Publishers, 1981), 124–27; and Wendell Garrett, *Victorian America: Classical Romanticism to Gilded Opulence* (New York: Universe Publishing, 1993), 110–17.

145. James Carnahan Wetmore, *The Wetmore Family of America* (Albany: Munsell and Rowland, 1861), 354–60; and Walter Barrett, *The Old Merchants of New York City* (New York: John W. Lovell Company, 1885), 2:292–301.

146. Henderson and Carlisle, *Marine Art and Antiques*, 107–13; Rina Prentice, *A Celebration of the Sea: The Decorative Art Collections of the National Maritime Museum* (United Kingdom: Her Majesty's Shipping Office, 1994), 66–67; Bea Howe, *Antiques from the Victorian Home* (New York: Charles Scribner's Sons, 1973), 214–16; Donald Berezoski, "Offshore Racer Unravels Anatomy of a Woolie," *Connoisseur's Quarterly* (2000): 60–63; and Mark Isaksen, *Woolies: Embroidered Ship Portraits*.

147. Michelle Tolini, "Sailor's Yarns: Nineteenth-Century Shipboard Needlework" (paper delivered at the Peabody Essex Museum's embroidery art symposium, 1998).

148. Lahikainen, *In the American Spirit*, 8; and Madelyn Moeller, *Nineteenth-Century Women Photographers: A New Dimension in Leisure* (Norwalk, Conn.: Lockwood-Mathews Mansion Museum, 1987), 45.

149. Shipping logbook of the brig *John Gilpin* for 1840 and 1841, Phillips Library, Peabody Essex Museum; Carl L. Crossman, *The Decorative Arts of the China Trade* (Woodbridge, Suffolk, England: Antique Collectors' Club, 1991), 381–82; Christina H. Nelson, *Directly from China: Export Goods for the American Market, 1784–1930* (Salem, Mass.: Peabody Museum of Salem, 1985), 103; and Anquetil, *Silk*, 14.

150. Ruth B. Phillips, *The Souvenir in Native North American Art from the Northeast, 1700–1900* (Seattle: University of Washington Press, 1998), 141.

151. Monroe et al., *Gifts of the Spirit*, 52, 209; and Margaret H. Swain, "Moose Hair Embroideries of Canada," *Country Life* (1967): 765.

152. Elizabeth Donaghy Garrett, *At Home: The American Family, 1750–1870* (New York: Harry N. Abrams, 1990), 54–60.

153. Thomas King, *Neo-Classical Furniture Designs: A Reprint of Thomas King's "Modern Style of Cabinet Work Exemplified," 1829* (New York: Dover Publications, 1995), 2, 73; Henry Wycoff Belknap, "Joseph True, Wood Carver of Salem, and His Account

Book," *Essex Institute Historical Collections* 78 (1942): 121; and Anne Farnam, "Essex County Furniture Carving: The Continuance of a Tradition," *Essex Institute Historical Collections* 116 (1980): 147–50.

154. Margaret Burke Clunie, "Joseph True and the Piecework System in Salem," *Antiques* 111 (1977): 1008–9.

155. Stephen Ebinger, *Joseph True, Salem Woodcarver* (master's thesis, State University of New York at Oneonta, Cooperstown Graduate Program, 1997); and Mrs. Arthur T. Wellman to Mrs. John Hassel, registrar, Essex Institute, 12 February 1975, Phillips Library, Peabody Essex Museum.

156. Katherine C. Grier, "Animal House: Pet Keeping in Urban and Suburban Households in the Northeast, 1850–1900," in *New England's Creature, 1400–1900* (Boston: Boston University for the Dublin Seminar for New England Folklife, 1995), 117, 119–21.

157. Barbara Morris, *Victorian Embroidery* (New York: Thomas Nelson and Sons, 1962), 21; Gervase Jackson-Stops, *The Treasure Houses of Britain: Five Hundred Years of Private Patronage and Art Collecting* (New Haven: Yale University Press and Washington: National Gallery of Art, 1985), 600–5; and Parker, *The Subversive Stitch*, 158–59.

158. Lambert, *The Hand-Book of Needlework*, 129–31; and Hope Hanley, *Needlepoint in America* (New York: Charles Scribner's Sons, 1969), 110–13.

159. King, *Neo-Classical Furniture Designs*, 3–6.

160. Morris, *Victorian Embroidery*, 22; and Candace Wheeler, *The Development of Embroidery in America* (New York: Harper and Brothers, 1921), ill.

161. Morris, *Victorian Embroidery*, 29.

162. "Obituary Notices," *Essex Institute Historical Collections* 14 (1887): 272–75.

163. Sally Kevill-Davies, *Yesterday's Children: The Antiques and History of Childcare* (Woodbridge, Suffolk, England: Antique Collectors' Club, 1991), 165–70, 267–76.

164. Morris, *Victorian Embroidery*, 32–40; Santina M. Levey, *Discovering Embroidery of the Nineteenth Century* (Princes Risborough, Aylesbury, Buckinghamshire: Shire Publications, 1977), 10, plate 8; Parker, *The Subversive Stitch*, 174–78; and Kevill-Davies, *Yesterday's Children*, 269–76.

165. John A. Wells, *The Peabody Story* (Salem, Mass.: Essex Institute, 1972).

166. Deutsch and Ring, "Homage to Washington in Needlework and Prints," 417–19.

167. John Trumbull, *Autobiography, Reminiscences and Letters of John Trumbull from 1756 to 1841* (New York: Wiley and Putnam, 1841), 166–67, 435–36; and Harbeson, *American Needlework*, 107–9.

168. Raffaella Serena, *Embroideries and Patterns from Nineteenth-Century Vienna* (Woodbridge, Suffolk, England: Antique Collectors' Club, 1998), 83–88; and Parker, *The Subversive Stitch*, 143–46.

169. Walter Frye Turner, comp., *Representative Men of Somerville, 1872–1898* (Boston, 1898), 92.

170. M. V. and Dorothy Brewington, *The Marine Paintings and Drawings in the Peabody Museum* (Salem, Mass.: Peabody Museum of Salem, 1981); and Denys Brook-Hart, *British Nineteenth-Century Marine Paintings* (Woodbridge, Suffolk, England: Antique Collectors' Club, 1974), 16–27.

171. Dorothy E. R. Brewington, *Dictionary of Marine Artists* (Salem, Mass: Peabody Museum of Salem and Mystic, Conn.: Mystic Seaport Museum, 1982), 416; and Anthony Peluso, "Thomas Willis: A Correct Picture of Any Vessel Guaranteed," *Maine Antiques Digest* 8, no. 11 (1980): 34a.

172. Frederick C. Matthews, *American Merchant Ships, 1850–1900* (Salem, Mass.: Marine Research Society, 1930), 206–7.

173. Morris, *Victorian Embroidery*, 20–21.

174. Bryant F. Tolles Jr. with Carolyn K. Tolles, *Architecture in Salem: An Illustrated Guide* (Salem, Mass.: Essex Institute, 1983), 176–77; and Garrett, *Victorian America*, 88–93.

175. Katherine C. Grier, *Culture and Comfort: People, Parlors, and Upholstery, 1850–1930* (Rochester, N.Y.: Strong Museum, 1988), 263–69.

176. Edgar de N. Mayhew and Minor Myers Jr., *A Documentary History of American Interiors from the Colonial Era to 1915* (New York: Charles Scribner's Sons, 1980), 181–92.

177. Grier, *Culture and Comfort*, 268.

178. Clarence Cook, *The House Beautiful* (1881; reprint, New York: Dover Publications, 1995), 111–28.

179. Constance Cary Harrison, *Women's Handiwork in Modern Homes* (New York: Charles Scribner's Sons, 1881), 16.

180. Beverly Gordon, "Cozy, Charming, and Artistic: Stitching Together the American Home," in *The Arts and the American Home, 1890–1930*, ed. Jessica H. Foy and Karal Ann Marling (Knoxville: University of Tennessee Press, 1994), 126; Linda P. Parry, *Textiles of the Arts and Crafts Movement* (London: Thames and Hudson, 1988), 29; *Art Needlework: A Complete Manual of Embroidery in Silks and Crewels* (New York: Ward Lock, 1882), 11; and Lucretia P. Hale, ed., *Art-Needlework for Decorative Embroidery: Guide to Embroidery in Crewels, Silks, Appliqué, etc.* (Boston: S. W. Tilton, 1879), 1–2.

181. Catherine E. Beecher and Harriet Beecher Stowe, *American Woman's Home; or, Principles of Domestic Science* (1869; reprint, Hartford, Conn.: Stowe-Day Foundation, 1991), 84–90.

182. Sophia Frances Anne Caulfield and Blanche C. Saward, *The Dictionary of Needlework: An Encyclopaedia of Artistic, Plain and Fancy Needlework* (1882; reprint, New York: Arno Press, 1972), 28–34; and Serena, *Embroideries and Patterns of Nineteenth-Century Vienna*, 80–88.

183. Grier, *Culture and Comfort*, 149–51, 168; Henry T. Williams and Mrs. C. S. Jones, *Beautiful Homes; or, Hints in Home Furnishings* (New York: Henry T. Williams, 1878), 66–67.

184. James D. McCabe, *The Illustrated History of the Centennial Exhibition, Held in Commemoration of the One Hundredth Anniversary of American Independence* (Philadelphia: National Publishing Company, 1876), 593; Gordon, "Cozy, Charming, and Artistic," 126; Parry, *Textiles of the Arts and Crafts Movement*, 29; and Morris, *Victorian Embroidery*, 123, 141.

185. Walsh, "The Language of Flowers in Nineteenth-Century American Painting," 518–31.

186. Grier, *Culture and Comfort*, 86–88.

187. Garrett, *At Home*, 59–60.

188. [T. Edward Parker], *Kensington Embroidery and the Colors of Flowers* (Lynn, Mass.: J. F. Ingalls, 1884), 32.

189. Caulfield and Saward, *The Dictionary of Needlework*, 14–15.

190. *Boston Journal*, 4 April 1884, in a scrapbook of biographical clippings, 30:209, Phillips Library, Peabody Essex Museum.

191. Salem city directories, 1893–1900.

192. Constance Cary Harrison, *Women's Handiwork in Modern Homes* (New York: Charles Scribner's Sons, 1881), 205.

193. Ibid., 69.

194. Mayhew and Myers, *A Documentary History of American Interiors*, 248–50.

195. Morris, *Victorian Embroidery*, 66–67; *Ornamental Stitches for Embroidery* (Lynn, Mass.: T. E. Parker, 1885); and [Parker], *Kensington Embroidery and the Colors of Flowers*, 48–52.

196. *Salem Evening News*, 28 August 1908.

197. Catherine Lynn, "Surface Ornament: Wallpapers, Carpets, Textiles, and Embroidery," in *In Pursuit of Beauty: Americans and the Aesthetic Movement* (New York: Rizzoli for the Metropolitan Museum of Art, 1986), 65–66; and Morris, *Victorian Embroidery*, 135–40.

198. Lynn, "Surface Ornament," 95–105; Anthea Callen, *Women Artists of the Arts and Crafts Movement* (New York: Pantheon Books, 1979), 95–135; and [Parker], *Kensington Embroidery and the Colors of Flowers*, 50.

199. Laurel Thatcher Ulrich, *The Age of Homespun* (New York: Alfred A. Knopf, scheduled for 2001); and American Decorative Arts Department files, Peabody Essex Museum. Camwood is a dyestuff made from the wood of a tree that produced tones of brown and purple.

200. Photography Department, Peabody Essex Museum.

201. Beverly Historical Society, Beverly, Massachusetts.

202. *Salem Evening News*, 13 March 1927.

203. Eliza Philbrick, "Spinning in the Olden Time," *The Essex Antiquarian* 1 (1897): 88.

204. Celia Betsky, "Inside the Past: The Interior and the Colonial Revival in American Art and Literature, 1860–1914," in Alan Axelrod, ed., *The Colonial Revival in America* (New York: W. W. Norton for the Henry Francis du Pont Winterthur Museum, 1985), 260–64.

205. Rev. Jacob Chapman, *Genealogy of the Philbrick and Philbrook Family Descended from Thomas Philbrick* (Exeter, N.H., 1886), 57, 97, 99; William Little, *History of the Town of Weare, New Hampshire, 1735–1888* (Lowell, Mass.: S. W. Huse, 1888), 971–72.

206. Gordon, "Cozy, Charming, and Artistic," 130–31.

207. *Embroidery Lessons with Colored Studies, 1899* (New London, Conn.: Brainerd and Armstrong, 1898), 35–36.

208. Mrs. L. Barton Wilson et al., eds., *Corticelli Home Needlework 1898: A Manual of Art Needlework Embroidery and Knitting* (Florence, Mass.: Nonotuck Silk Company, 1898).

209. Gordon, "Cozy, Charming, and Artistic," 125–26.

210. *Salem Evening News*, 9 February 1963.

211. Parry, *Textiles of the Arts and Crafts Movement*, 9–15; Nicola J. Shilliam, "Boston and the Society of Arts and Crafts: Textiles," in *Inspiring Reform: Boston's Arts and Crafts Movement* (Wellesley, Mass.: Davis Museum and Cultural Center, Wellesley College, 1997), 100–102.

212. Donald King and Santina Levey, *The Victoria and Albert Museum's Textile Collection: Embroidery in Britain from 1200 to 1750* (New York: Canopy Books, 1993), 11–13, 109–10.

213. Parry, *Textiles of the Arts and Crafts Movement*, 133–34.

214. Beverly Gordon, "Spinning Wheels, Samplers, and the Modern Priscilla: The Images and Paradoxes of Colonial Revival Needlework," *Winterthur Portfolio* 33 (1998): 179–80.

215. Salem city directories, 1893–1918; Tolles, *Architecture in Salem*, 187–88. Edith O. Morse was the daughter of Edward Sylvester Morse, a Japan scholar and a director of the Peabody Academy of Science.

216. Mary Harrod Northend, "The Renaissance of the Sampler," in *Samplers Old and New* (Philadelphia: Franklin Printing Company for Whitman's Sampler, 1923), 11–13, a reprint of the article that appeared in *International Studio* in 1923.

217. Edward S. Morse, "Henry Mason Brooks. A Memoir," *Essex Institute Historical Collections* 34 (1898): 219–31.

218. Northend, "The Renaissance of the Sampler," 11–13.

219. Paula Bradstreet Richter, "Stories from Her Needle: Colonial Revival Samplers of Mary Saltonstall Parker," in *Textiles in New England II: Four Centuries of Material Life* (Boston: Boston University Press for the Dublin Seminar for New England Folklife, publication anticipated in 2001).

220. Katherine F. Gauss, "Contemporary History in Cross-Stitch," *House Beautiful* 38 (1915): 136.

221. Harbeson, *American Needlework*, 174–82.

222. William Rhoads, "Colonial Revival in American Craft," in *Revivals! Diverse Traditions, 1920–1945*, Janet Karden, ed. (New York: Harry N. Abrams for the American Craft Museum, 1994), 50–51.

223. Richter, "Stories from Her Needle."

224. Rhoads, "Colonial Revival in American Craft," 50–51; Gordon, "Spinning Wheels, Samplers, and the Modern Priscilla," 176; Ring, *Girlhood Embroidery*, 45–63; and Harbeson, *American Needlework*, 130.

225. John Bunyan, *The Pilgrim's Progress* (New York: Penguin Books, 1987).

226. Ferguson, *Signs and Symbols in Christian Art*, 103, 117.

227. Anne Orr, *Cross Stitch Designs* (1915).

228. Richter, "Stories from Her Needle."

229. Gordon, "Cozy, Charming, and Artistic," 137–38; Harbeson, *American Needlework*, 188–91; 192–221; and Gordon, "Spinning Wheels, Samplers, and the Modern Priscilla," 184.

230. Bowen, "The Fishing Lady and Boston Common," 70–73; and Ring, *Girlhood Embroidery*, 44–45.

231. Parker, *The Subversive Stitch*, 202–4.

232. Entry form for the Fiftieth Anniversary Exhibition of the Society of Arts and Crafts in Boston in 1947 and other photographs and clippings, Stephen Phillips Trust House, Salem, Massachusetts.

233. Arthur Adams, "Memoirs of the Deceased Members of the New England Historic Genealogical Society," *New England Historical and Genealogical Register* 109 (1955): 225.

234. Karen Evans Ulehla, *The Society of Arts and Crafts, Boston Exhibition Record, 1897–1927* (Boston: Boston Public Library, 1981), 173.

235. *Boston Herald*, 24 April 1932; and Marilee Boyd Meyer, *Inspiring Reform: Boston's Arts and Crafts Movement* (Wellesley, Mass.: Davis Museum and Cultural Center, Wellesley College, 1997), 227. The Stephen Phillips Trust House in Salem, Massachusetts, owns a collection of ceramics made by Nannie Jenks Borden Phillips.

236. Orban, ed., *Fiberarts Design Book Six*, 6; and Smith, *Celebrating the Stitch: Contemporary Embroidery of North America*, 2–5.

237. Linda Behar, artist's statement for *Blanket: Wrapped in My Parents' Love*, November 2000, American Decorative Arts Department files, Peabody Essex Museum.

238. Orban, *Fiberarts Design Book Six*, 6.

239. Linda Behar, artist's statement for *Blanket: Wrapped in My Parents' Love*.

240. Nancy Stapen, "Coaxing the Unearthly from Terra Firma," *Boston Globe*, 28 September 1995; and Patricia Harris and David Lyon, "Linda Behar: Nature Compact," *American Craft* 58 (1998): 42–45.

241. "Nathaniel Rogers' General Store and School Account Book," 1789–94, Rogers Family Papers, Phillips Library, Peabody Essex Museum. Based on the piece's striking similarity to a number of coats of arms worked in Boston under Eleanor Druitt, Betty Ring suggests that Sally worked with her. It is not known at present whether there is a connection between the two schoolmistresses.

242. Not surprisingly, embroidered coats of arms gradually fell out of favor with girls in the late Federal period, although painted versions remained popular through the 1830s. See Betty Ring, "Heraldic Needlework of the Neoclassical Period," *Antiques* 144 (1993): 484–93.

243. These lessons were not always appreciated or enjoyed, as Sally's older cousin Lydia Nichols confirmed in 1799: "[I] cannot tell you anything about my Latin, only that it is tedious Stuff!!" This quotation is from Susan Nichols Pulsifer's *The Witch's Breed*, 188.

244. Nichols Family Papers, Phillips Library, Peabody Essex Museum. Benjamin was a student at Harvard College at the time.

245. Marshall Smelser was the first to label this period as an "Age of Passion" for the influence that strong emotions like hate, anger, and fear had on politics. I would add love to this list, based on the motivating forces behind Salem's school for scandal. See Marshall Smelser, "The Federalist Period as an Age of Passion," *American Quarterly* 10 (1958): 391.

246. Pulsifer, *The Witch's Breed*, 179.

247. George and Sally's mothers were sisters. A match between cousins was quite common among Salem elites at the time. See Bernard Farber's *Guardians of Virtue: Salem Families in 1800* (New York: Basic Books, 1972) for the economic and personal advantages of such a marriage.

248. Pulsifer, *The Witch's Breed*, 186.

249. Ibid., 191.

250. In addition to being class orator at his college commencement, Story was invited by his home town of Marblehead to speak on the occasion of George Washington's death.

251. Pulsifer, *The Witch's Breed*, 179.

252. One of Lydia's contemporaries and another pupil at the Rogers school, Susanna Holyoke mentions these events in her diary during the late 1790s. A transcription of the diary is among the Holyoke Family Papers, Phillips Library, Peabody Essex Museum.

253. For an account of their activities and Story's spontaneous wordplay, see William W. Story, *Life and Letters of Joseph Story* (Boston: Charles C. Little and James Brown, 1851), 88. The lengthy account written by "L," described as one of Story's "female friends, to whom he was warmly attached, and intimately known in early life," is almost certainly from Lydia. Story's letter to Lydia of 19 May 1802 describes the watchpaper. See Pulsifer, *The Witch's Breed*, 195.

254. Story, *Life and Letters of Joseph Story*, 86–87.

255. In 1785, an earlier social club named Sans Souci was formed by Harrison Gray Otis and his friends in Boston. The *Boston Centinel* published an attack by the Federalist Samuel Adams describing the club's introduction of cardplaying and refreshments to the Boston social scene as an act of dissipation, moral degeneracy, and effeminacy. See John Bixler Hench, *The Newspaper in a Republic: Boston's* Centinel *and* Chronicle, *1784–1801* (Ph.D. dissertation, Clark University, 1979), 153.

256. Wollstonecraft's most influential work, *A Vindication of the Rights of Women* (1792), was reprinted in America four times in two years and appeared in more private libraries than Thomas Paine's *The Rights of Man*, according to Chandos Michael Brown in "Mary Wollstonecraft; or, The Female Illuminati: The Campaign against Women and 'Modern Philosophy' in the Early Republic" [*Journal of the Early Republic* 13 (1995): 404]. John Dabney's *Catalogue of Books, for Sale or Circulation, in Town and Country* published in Salem in 1801 lists three works by Mary Wollstonecraft: "Essay on Education," "Rights of Woman," and "Maria, or, the Wrongs of Woman."

257. See Brown, "Mary Wollstonecraft" for a full analysis of how Wollstonecraft became a Federalist pariah.

258. Nichols Family Papers, Phillips Library, Peabody Essex Museum.

259. Ichabod Nichols to Lydia Nichols, 6 September 1800, as reprinted in Pulsifer, *The Witch's Breed*, 189–90.

260. "A Friend to Her Sex," *Salem Gazette*, 13 December 1800. Although Mrs. Rogers is not identified by name in the letter, William Bentley's diary and correspondence within the Nichols Family Papers make it clear that Salem residents knew she was the one under attack.

261. Benjamin F. Browne, "Youthful Recollections of Salem," *Essex Institute Historical Collections* 49 (1913): 206.

262. *Diary of the Reverend William Bentley,* 2:31.

263. George Granville Putnam, "Salem Vessels and Their Voyages," *Essex Institute Historical Collections* 65 (1929): 10.

264. Harrigan, "Schoolgirl Samplers of Federal Salem," 76–77; and *Diary of the Reverend William Bentley,* 2:31.

265. *Diary of the Reverend William Bentley,* 2:210.

266. Inventory of the estate of Nathaniel Rogers, probate records of Essex County, Massachusetts, 367:340.

267. Hench, *The Newspaper in a Republic,* 106. According to Hench, the *Centinel* had a circulation of 3,300 in 1795. In 1800, sixty percent of the subscribers lived outside the Boston area, in all states and several European countries.

268. *Salem Impartial Register,* 15 December 1800.

269. Lydia Nichols to Benjamin Peirce, May 1801, reprinted in Pulsifer, *The Witch's Breed,* 193.

270. *Diary of the Reverend William Bentley,* 2:360.

271. Samuel Roads Jr., *The History and Traditions of Marblehead* (Marblehead: N. Allen Lindsey, 1897), 261–62: "Girls as well as boys went to the same school at the same hours, and were arranged on opposite sides of a large hall on their appropriate forms. In the simplicity of those days it was not thought necessary to separate the sexes in their studies. Generally we studied the same books, and as we recited our lessons in the presence of each other, there was a mutual pride to do our best, and to gain an honest portion of flattery or praise. I was early struck with the flexibility, activity, and power of the female mind. Girls of the same age were on an average of numbers quite our equals in their studies and acquirements, and had much greater quickness of perception and delicacy of feeling than the boys. Remaining thus at school with them until I was about fifteen years old [1794], I could not be mistaken as to their powers; and I then imbibed the opinion, which I have never since changed, that their talents are generally equal to those of men, though there are shades of difference in the character of their minds resulting from several causes."

272. "Joseph Story to Lydia N," later attributed to 1801, Joseph Story Papers, Harvard University Archives.

273. The most recent biography of Justice Story is that of R. Kent Newmyer, *Supreme Court Justice: Joseph Story, Statesman of the Old Republic* (Chapel Hill: University of North Carolina Press, 1985).

274. Benjamin Peirce to Joseph Story, June 1827, Harvard Archives.

275. Benjamin Peirce Papers, Harvard Archives.

276. "Bentley's Record of Deaths," *Essex Institute Historical Collections* 19 (1880): 95.

277. *Index of Obituaries in* Massachusetts Centinel *and* Columbian Centinel, *1784–1840* (Boston: G. K. Hall, 1961), 4:3864.

278. [Benjamin Silliman], *Letters of Shahcoolen, a Hindu Philosopher, Residing in Philadelphia; To His Friend El Hassan, an Inhabitant of Delhi* (Boston: Russell and Cutler, 1802), 47; and *Diary of the Reverend William Bentley,* 2:405. The anonymous letters were later bound and published by Russell, printer of the Boston *Columbian Centinel,* and Silliman was eventually identified as the author. Bentley identified Mrs. Rogers as this unnamed woman in his diary, raging that "the vile slanders propagated last year to injure a school mistress in this Town have been echoed from other parts of the Continent" through Shahcoolen's attack.

279. Letter to the editor from "Luric," *Impartial Register,* 3 December 1801. Quite possibly, Bentley himself wrote the letter.

Painted with Thread: **The Art of American Embroidery**
Designed in ITC Giovanni Book by Bohoy Design, Beverly
Farms, Massachusetts
Printed by The Stinehour Press, Lunenburg, Vermont
Bound by Acme Bookbinding, Charlestown, Massachusetts